OPPOSING
VIEWPOINTS®
SERIES

The Achievement Gap

Other Books of Related Interest:

Opposing Viewpoints Series

Education

At Issue Series

Has No Child Left Behind Been Good for Education?

Current Controversies Series

Homeschooling

"Congress shall make
no law . . . abridging
the freedom of speech,
or of the press."

First Amendment to the U.S. Constitution

The basic foundation of our democracy is the First Amendment guarantee of freedom of expression. The Opposing Viewpoints Series is dedicated to the concept of this basic freedom and the idea that it is more important to practice it than to enshrine it.

OPPOSING VIEWPOINTS® SERIES

The Achievement Gap

Karen Miller, Book Editor

GREENHAVEN PRESS
A part of Gale, Cengage Learning

GALE
CENGAGE Learning™

Detroit • New York • San Francisco • New Haven, Conn • Waterville, Maine • London

Christine Nasso, *Publisher*
Elizabeth Des Chenes, *Managing Editor*

For more information, contact:
Greenhaven Press
27500 Drake Rd.
Farmington Hills, MI 48331-3535
Or you can visit our Internet site at gale.cengage.com

Articles in Greenhaven Press anthologies are often edited for length to meet page requirements. In addition, original titles of these works are changed to clearly present the main thesis and to explicitly indicate the author's opinion. Every effort is made to ensure that Greenhaven Press accurately reflects the original intent of the authors. Every effort has been made to trace the owners of copyrighted material.

Cover Image copyright Adam Gault/Photodisc/Getty Images.

LIBRARY OF CONGRESS CATALOGING-IN-PUBLICATION DATA

The achievement gap / Karen Miller, book editor.
      p. cm. -- (Opposing viewpoints)
    Includes bibliographical references and index.
    ISBN 978-0-7377-4749-2 (hardcover) -- ISBN 978-0-7377-4750-8 (pbk.)
    1. Academic achievement--United States--Juvenile literature. 2. Educational equalization--United States--Juvenile literature. I. Miller, Karen, 1973-
      LB1062.6.A33 2010
      379.2'60973--dc22
                                                              2010000262

Printed in the United States of America
2 3 4 5 6 7 14 13 12 11 10

Contents

Chapter 3: What Educational Strategies Narrow the Achievement Gap?

Chapter 4: How Does Public Policy Affect the Achievement Gap?

Why Consider Opposing Viewpoints?

"The only way in which a human being can make some approach to knowing the whole of a subject is by hearing what can be said about it by persons of every variety of opinion and studying all modes in which it can be looked at by every character of mind. No wise man ever acquired his wisdom in any mode but this."

John Stuart Mill

In our media-intensive culture it is not difficult to find differing opinions. Thousands of newspapers and magazines and dozens of radio and television talk shows resound with differing points of view. The difficulty lies in deciding which opinion to agree with and which "experts" seem the most credible. The more inundated we become with differing opinions and claims, the more essential it is to hone critical reading and thinking skills to evaluate these ideas. Opposing Viewpoints books address this problem directly by presenting stimulating debates that can be used to enhance and teach these skills. The varied opinions contained in each book examine many different aspects of a single issue. While examining these conveniently edited opposing views, readers can develop critical thinking skills such as the ability to compare and contrast authors' credibility, facts, argumentation styles, use of persuasive techniques, and other stylistic tools. In short, the Opposing Viewpoints Series is an ideal way to attain the higher-level thinking and reading skills so essential in a culture of diverse and contradictory opinions.

In addition to providing a tool for critical thinking, Opposing Viewpoints books challenge readers to question their own strongly held opinions and assumptions. Most people form their opinions on the basis of upbringing, peer pressure, and personal, cultural, or professional bias. By reading carefully balanced opposing views, readers must directly confront new ideas as well as the opinions of those with whom they disagree. This is not to simplistically argue that everyone who reads opposing views will—or should—change his or her opinion. Instead, the series enhances readers' understanding of their own views by encouraging confrontation with opposing ideas. Careful examination of others' views can lead to the readers' understanding of the logical inconsistencies in their own opinions, perspective on why they hold an opinion, and the consideration of the possibility that their opinion requires further evaluation.

Evaluating Other Opinions

To ensure that this type of examination occurs, Opposing Viewpoints books present all types of opinions. Prominent spokespeople on different sides of each issue as well as well-known professionals from many disciplines challenge the reader. An additional goal of the series is to provide a forum for other, less known, or even unpopular viewpoints. The opinion of an ordinary person who has had to make the decision to cut off life support from a terminally ill relative, for example, may be just as valuable and provide just as much insight as a medical ethicist's professional opinion. The editors have two additional purposes in including these less known views. One, the editors encourage readers to respect others' opinions—even when not enhanced by professional credibility. It is only by reading or listening to and objectively evaluating others' ideas that one can determine whether they are worthy of consideration. Two, the inclusion of such viewpoints encourages the important critical thinking skill of objectively evaluating an author's credentials and bias. This evaluation will illuminate an author's reasons for taking a particular stance on an issue and will aid in readers' evaluation of the author's ideas.

It is our hope that these books will give readers a deeper understanding of the issues debated and an appreciation of the complexity of even seemingly simple issues when good and honest people disagree. This awareness is particularly important in a democratic society such as ours in which people enter into public debate to determine the common good. Those with whom one disagrees should not be regarded as enemies but rather as people whose views deserve careful examination and may shed light on one's own.

Thomas Jefferson once said that "difference of opinion leads to inquiry, and inquiry to truth." Jefferson, a broadly educated man, argued that "if a nation expects to be ignorant and free ... it expects what never was and never will be." As individuals and as a nation, it is imperative that we consider the opinions of others and examine them with skill and discernment. The Opposing Viewpoints Series is intended to help readers achieve this goal.

David L. Bender and Bruno Leone,
Founders

Introduction

"We have to ensure that we're educating and preparing our people for the new jobs of the 21st century. We've got to prepare our people with the skills they need to compete in this global economy. Time and again, when we placed our bet for the future on education, we have prospered as a result—by tapping the incredible innovative and generative potential of a skilled American workforce."

—President Barack Obama,
Remarks on the American
Graduation Initiative, delivered to
Macomb Community College
(Warren, MI), July 14, 2009.

Data from the 2006 Programme for International Student Assessment (PISA) reveal that fifteen-year-olds in the United States ranked fifteenth of twenty-nine nations studied by the Organisation for Economic Co-operation and Development (OECD) on tests of reading literacy, twenty-first on tests of scientific literacy, and twenty-fifth in mathematics literacy. As stated in the study, the highest-achieving students can compete with students from any nation in the world, but the difference in performance between the highest- and lowest-achieving students in the United States is greater than in any other nation in the study. According to the U.S. Census Bureau, the minority groups that disproportionately produce the low-achieving students will make up half of the U.S. population by 2050; if the nation does not find a way to improve its students' basic communication and scientific skills soon, many believe the United States will lose its competitive edge completely.

Not everyone agrees with the conclusions drawn from this data, however. Clifford Adelman, author of the Institute for Higher Education Policy's report *The Spaces Between Numbers: Getting International Data on Higher Education Straight*, argues that the comparisons made by the OECD in its report, *Education at a Glance 2008*, are not as straightforward as they appear. For example, "tertiary" education may refer sometimes to any higher education, the completion of two-year degrees, or the completion of four-year degrees. Although the differences are explained in lengthy footnotes and appendices, it is too easy for a journalist or policy maker to glance at a table and come to the wrong conclusion. Adelman's interpretation of the data suggests that American adults are as educated and successful as any in the world; if an achievement gap does exist between American high school students and their international peers, it closes as they grow up.

Adelman's report, however, is not without critics. "Data on U.S. College Degrees Called Misleading," a 2009 article by Debra Viadero in *Education Week*, presents several arguments against his optimistic conclusions about the state of higher education in the United States. Terry Hartle, a senior vice president of the American Council on Education (ACE), acknowledges that American young adults (age 25) do lag behind young adults in other nations for college degree attainment, and the number has been slipping each year. Considering the relatively poor performance of American high school students on the PISA assessments, it seems reasonable to expect the achievement gap between young Americans and their peers to widen. Even without comparing the education levels of Americans to people in other countries, Hartle addresses other reasons to be disappointed in these numbers. "If we want people to get the most personal value from a postsecondary degree and we want the most societal benefits," he says in the article, "it would be better if people got a degree at 25 than 55."

Andreas Schleicher, head of the Indicators and Analysis Division in the Directorate for Education of the OECD, sees almost no value in Adelman's conclusions about the disparities in higher education between the United States and the rest of the world. "There are so many fundamental conceptual flaws in the argumentation [of Adelman's report]," he says, that it does not even "warrant a serious response." In *Understanding and Reporting on Academic Rigor*, a "primer for journalists" published by the Hechinger Institute on Education and the Media at the Teachers College at Columbia University, Schleicher points to structural differences in the U.S. educational system that put American students at an explicit disadvantage to students of other nations. He says that "the highest-performing countries apply rigorous academic standards, recruit and train top-notch teachers, dig deeply into the subject matter, and allow little variance in performance by the highest- and lowest-performing schools." In contrast, American schools cover too many topics too thinly, have too much variation by state, and tolerate the vast differences in school performance across social and economic status lines, even among schools in the same district. Because the United States has no real national control of teaching methods and curriculum standards (current assessments come from standardized test scores that do not directly measure teacher performance, only student performance), it can have no national standards of teaching methodology and performance and no national plans for improvement.

These global differences in achievement are analogous to the differences in achievement between students from various states, cities, and even neighborhoods: Some schools consistently perform well while others have always struggled to serve their student populations. *Opposing Viewpoints: The Achievement Gap* examines these schools as well as how belonging to certain groups—such as race, economic circumstance, or natural ability—affects students' academic achievement and what solutions have been devised to increase their opportunities for success. The book's four chapters, What Causes the Achievement Gap? How Do Schools Affect the Achievement Gap? What Educational Strategies Narrow the Achievement Gap? and How Does Public Policy Affect the Achievement Gap? address some of the social and economic problems that arise from the achievement gap, examine the success of a variety of approaches to those problems, and speculate about how the current achievement gap could affect the future of the nation.

OPPOSING VIEWPOINTS® SERIES

CHAPTER 1

What Causes the Achievement Gap?

Chapter Preface

Khadijah Williams, class of 2009, earned admission and received a full scholarship to Harvard University. Harvard is a very competitive, very prestigious school, but she was not the first student from Los Angeles—or even from Jefferson High School—to do be admitted there, nor will she be the last. Admission on scholarship is impressive but not in itself remarkable. What makes her achievement so extraordinary is that she graduated from high school at all. The daughter of a homeless woman, Williams learned from standardized test results in third grade not only that she was considered gifted, but also that a good education could prepare her for a safe, stable life. Williams's family moved around Southern California her entire life, so she switched schools frequently and sometimes missed entire years, but her junior year she made the decision to stay at one school until graduation, even after her mother and sister left the area; she would wake up at 4:00 A.M. for the bus ride from Orange County to Los Angeles and would not return to her family until nearly midnight. Once, when she returned to their shelter during her senior year, she found that her family had left her behind. Nonetheless, with help from teachers and mentors, she applied to colleges, participated in the California Academic Decathlon, ran track and field, and graduated at age eighteen with the rest of her class. Despite many challenges, she has managed to achieve more than many students ever do.

The "achievement gap" is a distressing puzzle to academics, politicians, educators, and even parents: Why some children acquire better educations than others and why there are so many differences between groups of children are complicated problems with too many variables, even when achievement seems to be easily classified by race or socioeconomic status. Poverty, for example, is often cited as an example of why students lag behind in school; one explanation suggests that students from poor families have responsibilities (e.g., child care and wage earning) that take up time students from wealthier families can spend on academics. Race is another common explanation, and its proponents assert that discrimination or cultural differences affect how students feel or are treated within school systems and in later job markets. Innate intelligence is considered a reasonable explanation by some researchers; family experience and education level equally so by others. Because all of these factors influence each other, however, no clear paths to attaining success for all students exist.

Khadijah Williams's story is a profound lesson on the power of individual determination and accomplishment. Finding food and safety and keeping clean while living on the streets are monumental tasks, and children are especially vulnerable to physical and environmental dangers. Most impoverished students still have homes to live in and can be reasonably assured that if they put a textbook on a table at night it will be there in the morning. Williams is black, but the American educational and employment landscapes are filled with members of all races and ethnicities in positions of power and affluence; she will not be noted for her skin color when she begins college or embarks on her career. Although her mother had no information to share with her about how to navigate through a school system or apply to universities and for scholarships, Williams reached out to teachers and other adults who did. That she has been labeled as a gifted, intelligent person is not irrelevant to her academic achievement, but even if she had earned only a high school diploma she still would have been equipped for a much better life as an adult than she had as a child. By achieving so much with so little, she provides proof that membership in a traditionally low-achieving group does not necessarily limit how much an individual can accomplish and raises questions about whether achievement gaps are social or personal phenomena.

The following chapter explores some of the explanations for the differences in academic and professional achievement among racial and social groups and some solutions proposed for mitigating the gap and eliminating the economic inequalities that arise as a consequence.

> "It's time to acknowledge and address
> the achievement gap between white and
> minority students in their schools and
> across the country."

Racial Differences Contribute to the Achievement Gap

Melissa Jenco

Melissa Jenco is a staff writer at the Daily Herald, *a daily newspaper serving the ninety communities that make up the suburbs of Chicago, Illinois. The following viewpoint focuses on two schools that have implemented race-based intervention programs to help black and Hispanic students—who make up the minority of the student population in these mostly white environments— score as well on college entrance exams and core academic subjects as their white and Asian classmates do. Race-based programs are controversial, but their defenders say that students of different groups have different problems, and it makes sense to offer different solutions.*

As you read, consider the following questions:

1. As cited by the author, how does the performance of black students as a group on state standardized tests compare to their white and Asian counterparts?

2. According to minority academic achievement consultant Lourdes Ferrer, what factors contribute to the relatively poor performance of minority students in school?

3. What are some of the non-math topics addressed in the all-black ACT preparation class at Waubonsie Valley High School?

Two area high schools [in Illinois] are trying a new approach to bolster test scores for struggling black and Hispanic students by offering them additional assistance programs aimed almost entirely at minorities.

Leaders at Neuqua Valley and Waubonsie Valley high schools in Indian Prairie Unit District 204 say it's time to acknowledge and address the achievement gap between white and minority students in their schools and across the country.

And part of that, they say, is to admit that people of different races and cultures aren't all the same and may learn differently.

"(People of color) look in the mirror and see color, so we should see color and also acknowledge that and know that person is coming from a different experience," Neuqua principal Mike Popp said. "We should recognize that and then we should make sure we're being sensitive to the way this person learns."

At Waubonsie Valley in Aurora, students now can take a new all-black ACT [college entrance exam] prep course. At Neuqua Valley in Naperville, black and Hispanic students can get help with their homework from other minority students through the Face to Face program.

Students who are not minorities are not barred from either of the groups, but they aren't targeted by teachers to participate, either. And not all students invited to join the program do so. Less than half of the 60 students who were invited to be part of the all-black ACT prep course accepted the offer.

Assessing Black Students as a Group

During each of the past five years, black students were the lowest-scoring racial subgroup on standardized tests at both schools.

At Waubonsie, on average, only about 29.6 percent of black students met or exceeded state standards in math during that period and only 38.5 percent met or exceeded standards in reading.

During the same period, on average, 72.7 percent of white students met or exceeded standards in math and 74.1 percent met or exceeded them in reading. Scores for Asians showed 84.3 percent met or exceeded standards in math and 78.1 percent in reading.

At Neuqua, about 47.7 percent of black students on average met state math standards while 54.9 percent met standards in reading.

On average, 77.8 percent of white students met standards in both math and reading. Among Asian students, an average of about 83.8 percent met math standards and 76 percent met reading standards.

The achievement gap is not a new phenomenon, but educators say they hesitated in the past to treat any student or group differently based in race.

Now, they say, the problem has continued too long to ignore.

"We've always been afraid to target an audience because some people, some constituents, would think it's not appropriate. But, yeah, you need to do that," Waubonsie principal Jim Schmid said.

Reasons for the Achievement Gap

For years, researchers have been studying the root causes of the gap in test scores between races. Lourdes Ferrer, English Language Learners and minority academic achievement consultant for the DuPage Regional Office of Education, has interviewed dozens of minority students about why they think their scores are lower than their white and Asian peers.

She says there are a variety of factors at play, including parents who may not be able to help because they themselves are uneducated or can't negotiate today's educational system.

Low self-esteem, low expectations and a lack of minority role models also tend to play into the equation, Ferrer said.

In addition, some black and Hispanic families may have different standards for academic success or different educational priorities, she said.

Many Hispanic families, for example, come to the United States for jobs and may see work—and not education—as the way out of poverty.

"If parents have not had the chance to succeed in school, it's harder for them to coach their children's academic life," Ferrer said. "It's clear the community understands (minority) parents love their children, but love sometimes is not enough to be a coach."

For Hispanic students, language barriers also may be an issue, she said.

All-Black ACT Preparation Class

Waubonsie math teacher Natalie Johnson, who is black, started the school's all-black ACT prep class this fall after seeing year after year of consistently low scores from some black students.

"These students are not being successful for whatever reason, so the only way to figure out why they're not being successful is to isolate them and get to the root causes," she said.

"It's irresponsible to sit back and think everybody else will fix it."

How the Culture of Cool Can Undermine Black Male Achievement

Although black males have developed multiple survival techniques throughout their history in the United States, the "cool pose" is perhaps unique. This pose, a ritualized form of masculinity, uses certain behavior, scripts, physical posturing, and carefully crafted performance to convey a strong impression of pride, strength, and control. The cool pose is a coping mechanism to hide self-doubt, insecurity, and inner turmoil, and can be observed in such things as dress (for example, beltless pants hanging below the waist), manner of talk (signifying, rapping), and behavior (high fives, special handshakes, forms of greeting). The black male adopts the cool pose as a way to:

• Cope with oppression, invisibility, and marginality.

• Communicate power, toughness, detachment, and style.

• Maintain a balance between his inner life and his social environment.

• Cope with conflict and anxiety.

• Render him visible and empower him.

• Neutralize stress.

• Manage his feelings of rage in the face of prejudice and discrimination.

• Counter the negative forces in his life.

Alfred W. Tatum,
Teaching Reading to Black Adolescent Males.
Portland, ME: Stenhouse Publishers, 2005.

In addition to learning the four basic skills on the ACT—math, science, English and reading—the 20 students in the class also talk about responsibility, leadership and self-discipline, as well as changing the negative perceptions people may have about them.

In a recent class discussion, students were talking about their goals and the importance of finishing high school and going to college. One student said his goal is to be a rapper.

"(Education) increases your chances, Mr. 'I'm going to get my GED [General Educational Development] and my goal is to make money,'" Johnson told him. "Well, you know what? There's a whole lot of people who are going to be rappers out there. What are you going to do to put yourself head and shoulders above people who say 'I'm going to be a rapper?'"

Students in the class say when they heard how far behind black students were performing on state tests, they thought they might be able to help improve the group's overall score.

Darrell Echols, dean of students at the school, has a daughter in the class and said he trusts Johnson and her instructional style. He believes if other interventions aren't helping to raise scores, it's time to try something new.

Echols said about 13 percent of the school is black. Many of the students were not raised in District 204 and are not used to being in a predominantly white environment. Being in an all-black class gives them an extra comfort level.

Junior Amber Sykes agrees and said she likes the open discussions and participation the class offers.

"We talk about things we're going through and how people perceive African Americans and try to stereotype us," she said. "We just talk about a lot of things. A lot of things . . . we won't say it to any other teacher but if she (Johnson) asks us we'd be open-minded and tell her about stuff. It's like a big family."

Johnson says no one should think that comfortable atmosphere somehow translates into lax standards.

27

"Setting expectations will help them realize their potential and jump up and reach that bar," she said. "It's not going to be lowered."

The Face to Face Program

Last year, Neuqua teachers started a minority tutoring program called Face to Face in response to feedback from students at a diversity forum who talked about a lack of minority role models.

Roughly 25 black and Hispanic students serve as tutors twice a week after school to provide academic support and to be mentors to their peers. Teachers recommend students both to be tutors and to get help from tutors.

Diane Tancredi, one of the group's founders, echoed the view that minority students feel comfortable working with each other and said it actually lessens racial tensions.

"They're not seeking help from white kids who know more than (they do)," she said. "It's their peer, their cultural identity. It's someone from their culture who is successful and says, 'yes, you can do this.'"

Two students who were tutored last year [2008] have returned this year, but this time as tutors.

Senior Julius "Trey" Bedford, one of the group's tutors, said there's sometimes a different mind-set among minority students in a predominantly white high school.

"It's really easier to fall back into the background," he said. "But we tried to use resources through leadership sessions just to kind of convey that it's OK to do well, it's OK to try hard at school ... try to make the most of what you have at Neuqua because it's your school as much as anyone else's."

Racial Targeting Is Not Segregation

With America's history of slavery followed by segregation, Ferrer acknowledges that targeting certain races for specific types of help may trigger some controversy.

But she applauds the two schools for taking a risk she sees as targeting, not segregating.

"I think what they're doing is targeting groups of students that have specific needs and challenges and providing services to get them to proficiency," she said.

> "Our personal observations and experi-
> ences with diverse populations of stu-
> dents told us that the achievement gap
> was not a matter of race or ethnicity,
> but rather a question of personal chal-
> lenges faced by individual students."

Racial Differences
Do Not Contribute to
the Achievement Gap

Al Ramirez and Dick Carpenter

Al Ramirez and Dick Carpenter are associate professors in the Department of Leadership, Research, and Foundations at the University of Colorado at Colorado Springs. The following viewpoint, the second part of a two-paper research project on the achievement gap, explores whether the gap has a racial component and how educational leaders can fall into the trap of thinking it is a white/minority problem. Ramirez and Carpenter ultimately argue that there are more differences than similarities in achievement within racial and ethnic groups, and that race is not a significant indicator of the likelihood of a student dropping out of school.

Al Ramirez and Dick Carpenter, "The Matter of Dropouts," *Phi Delta Kappan*, vol. 90, May 2009, pp. 656–659. Copyright © 2009 Phi Delta Kappa, Inc. Reproduced by permission of the publisher and the authors.

As you read, consider the following questions:

1. In their first study of the achievement gap, what did the viewpoint authors discover about minority groups and achievement?

2. What are some shared predictors of student dropout rates or school success among white, black, and Hispanic students, as indicated by the authors?

3. Why do the viewpoint authors warn against perceiving the achievement gap as a matter of differences between white students as a group and minority students as a group?

As an educational researcher, it's gratifying to wonder about some problem of practice, undertake a systematic investigation, and discover that your speculation or gut feeling about the issue proved right. This has been the case in our study of achievement gaps. Although today we are university professors with responsibilities for teaching and scholarship, other career experiences as teachers and school administrators also shaped our perspective on education. We questioned much of the research literature about the achievement gap between minority and majority students. Our personal observations and experiences with diverse populations of students told us that the achievement gap was not a matter of race or ethnicity, but rather a question of personal challenges faced by individual students. We believe that the key to policy development related to overcoming the achievement gap is more likely to be found by understanding differences within groups rather than between groups.

In our first study, reported in "Challenging Assumptions About the Achievement Gap," we presented our findings from an examination of student achievement among black, Hispanic (or Latino), and white students. That research determined that the singular definition of "achievement gap" (that is, the difference between white and minority students) misrepresents the complex and multilayered dynamics at work in the academic achievement of black, Hispanic, and white students. Instead of the dominant and singular understanding of "the" achievement gap, we demonstrated that there are multiple gaps related to student achievement and that the more significant achievement gaps were not between groups, but within groups. We concluded that casting the achievement gap as a white/minority dichotomy was a risky misconception that potentially promotes poor policy solutions. That research was based on an analysis of data from the National Educational Longitudinal Study of 1988.

We recently expanded our achievement gap research beyond the typical measure of student performance on tests to high school dropout status. Once again, we looked at data from black, Hispanic, and white student cohorts using the National Educational Longitudinal Study of 1988. As in our earlier research, we examined differences in dropout status both between and within racial/ethnic groups, paying particular attention to differences or similarities in significant predictors for each group. Moreover, we explored whether the predictor variables for the three groups in our earlier study would also predict dropout behavior in the same manner. We found that the patterns of significant predictors for dropout status were not the same as in the earlier study, and in the process we uncovered a new set of variables associated with dropping out. Yet, the new set of significant predictors for dropout status did demonstrate some consistency with our earlier research. We found certain common patterns among white and Hispanic students, but we found no statistically significant differences in dropout status based on race/ethnicity. Thus, once again we found that within-group differences may be more significant than between-group differences.

Challenging Conventional Wisdom About the Achievement Gap

The overall thrust of our research has been to challenge the conventional wisdom about the achievement gap, which is typically characterized as a difference in learning between white and minority students. In our first study of achievement gaps, we looked at academic achievement and found not one but many gaps, and the most significant of these gaps existed within the racial and ethnic groups themselves. That study tested a large index of predictor variables for each racial/ethnic group and identified these as the most significant:

- Socioeconomic status (for all three groups);

- Participation in an English language acquisition program (for all three groups);

- Time spent on homework (for black and white students);

- Number of units of algebra taken (for Hispanic and white students); and

- Level of parent involvement (for all three groups). . . .

As in our first study, we found race/ethnicity was not a significant predictor of dropping out. We also discovered substantive, but not perfect, overlap in predictor variables between Hispanic and white students. For white students, going to a school with more minority students, facing increased gang activity, being suspended more often, having siblings who drop out, and being held back all increase the likelihood of dropping out. More time on homework, more time in extracurricular activities, higher math scores in 10th grade, being a male, having two parents at home, and more parental involvement decrease the likelihood of dropping out for white students. For black students, more suspensions, inclusion in ESL [English as a second language], and being held back increase the likelihood of dropping out, while increased parental involvement decreases it. For Hispanic students, more suspensions, inclusion in a dropout program, and being held back increase the likelihood of dropping out, while more time on homework, being a male, taking more units of Algebra 1, and having two parents in the house decreases the likelihood.

With the additional variables, all three groups share two variables in common—being held back and number of suspensions. For all groups, the relationship is the same—being held back and having more suspensions increase the likelihood of dropping out. In addition to those two variables, white and Hispanic students share four more variables—inclusion in a dropout program, time spent on homework, family composition, and gender. Again, the relationship is the same for both groups—inclusion in a dropout program and being a female increase the likelihood of dropping out, and living in two-parent homes and spending more time on homework decrease the likelihood of dropping out. Altogether, white and Hispanic students share six common predictors; white and black students share three common predictors; and black and Hispanic students share two common predictors.

How Educators Can Use These Findings

Our study of dropouts serves to underscore the findings from our prior study on achievement gaps. First, there are many gaps related to dropout behavior, not just one gap that explains the differences between white and minority student dropout rates. As such, we caution school leaders and policy makers about one-size-fits-all dropout prevention programs. What should be clear from the two studies is that policy should account for the differences we identify and allow sufficient flexibility at the school level for educators to craft interventions that suit local conditions and circumstances.

Second, the two studies also point to the folly of searching for magic bullets and simple quick fixes, which are the bane of

Even within a Single State, Districts with Similar Demographics can Have Different Levels of Achievement.

Four urban districts in Texas with similar poverty levels and ethnic/racial concentrations ...

Demographic category	District 1	District 2	District 3	District 4
County	County A	County A	County B	County C
Total size	59,000	203,000	159,000	79,457
Black	31%	29%	29%	26%
Latino	64%	60%	65%	58%
Economically disadvantaged	80%	80%	85%	69%

... but District 1 has a consistently higher achievement and lower dropout rate than others

TAKS all tests taken, 2008
% passing

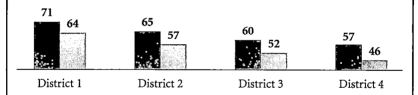

District 1	District 2	District 3	District 4

Annual dropout rate, grades 7–12, 2008
% of total

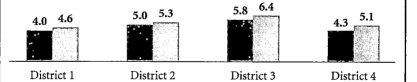

District 1	District 2	District 3	District 4

■ All students   ☐ Black students

TAKEN FROM: McKinsey and Company, *The Economic Impact of the Achievement Gap in America's Schools*, April 2009. www.mckinsey.com.

public education. Such approaches serve only to feed the cynicism about the effectiveness of precollegiate education in America. The one-size-fits-all model in the case of "the" achievement gap is a classic example of fad chasing, which is destructive because its inevitable failure only discourages educators, students, parents, and all stakeholders. Quick fixes discourage efforts to initiate change because of the enervating [weakening or destroying] effects that sap the energy and enthusiasm of those asked to engage in yet another fad promulgated by school leaders and policy makers.

Finally, we believe that efforts to mitigate the dropout crisis should be less concerned with the different factors between white and minority students, and more concerned with the dynamics affecting each subgroup or, better yet, groups of students in individual schools or school districts. Conceptualizing achievement gaps only as differences between white and minority students inaccurately treats the latter as a monolith—as if all minority students are the same. In fact, as our research consistently demonstrates, there are important differences between black and Hispanic students, and the latter arguably share more in common with white students than with black students. But even then, we caution that our research shows that these issues are less about race and ethnicity or socioeconomic status than about factors affecting students in different circumstances. Thinking of black, Hispanic, and white students as stereotypes that require unique group treatments is a mistake. The importance of within-group differences compared to between-group differences means teachers, leaders, and policy makers should extend uniqueness of treatment to the individual level, based on the student's personal needs and the professional judgment of the educators who work with him or her. As such, we believe the concept of within-group differences holds the key to successful intervention policy and programs.

We started our April 2005 *Kappan* article on achievement gaps with a metaphor from nature here in Colorado where we live. We end this article similarly to underscore the main point. Fifty-four peaks in the Colorado Rockies reach more than 14,000 feet in elevation, and many locals and visitors to the state climb these mountains as a form of personal challenge and recreation. About a third of these peaks are easy hikes that require merely a good set of lungs and a bit of stamina. Another third involve a more strenuous climb, and the last third require technical knowledge and equipment to ascend. Some of the peaks in the last group are very dangerous places that should be approached only by experts. To the casual observer looking from the valley, the 54 peaks appear remarkably similar, but understanding the considerable differences within this group is critical to would-be climbers. This same admonition about understanding the differences within groups applies to policy leaders as they address achievement gaps.

"While their children are still in the crib, higher-SES parents begin to push them in directions that put them in good shape for the kinds of questioning, analytic minds they will need as professionals and high-level managers."

Members of Higher Social Classes Have an Academic Edge

Richard E. Nisbett

Richard E. Nisbett is a distinguished university professor at the University of Michigan, Ann Arbor. He has written numerous books on intelligence and cultural psychology. The following viewpoint is excerpted from his book, Intelligence and How to Get It: Why Schools and Cultures Count, *which puts forth the idea that intelligence quotient, or IQ, is determined mostly by environment and very little by genetics. Nisbett argues that children from higher social and economic classes have an advantage from birth over their peers from poor or working-class families, because professional, middle-class parents teach even very young children the intellectual habits they need for school success.*

As you read, consider the following questions:

1. According to the author, how does how often professional and working-class parents speak to their children affect the size of the vocabulary that their children use?

2. How do professional and working-class families use words differently during ordinary, daily activities, such as playing games or making dinner, as cited by the author?

3. How do breaks from school, especially during the summer, affect skill and knowledge retention of children from the professional and working classes, according to Nisbett?

Higher-SES [socioeconomic status] people start preparing their children for life in the fast lane early on. While their children are still in the crib, higher-SES parents begin to push them in directions that put them in good shape for the kinds of questioning, analytic minds they will need as professionals and high-level managers. Lower-SES people are not raising doctors and CEOs; they are raising children who will eventually be workers whose obedience and good behavior will stand them in good stead with employers who are not looking to be second-guessed or evaluated.

Psychologists Betty Hart and Todd Risley of the University of Kansas carried out an extremely ambitious study of the differences in verbal behavior directed toward children among white professional people, working-class blacks and whites, and underclass, welfare blacks. They observed children and their parents in their homes for many hours. In this [viewpoint] I will focus on the differences between professional and working-class families.

Professional parents talk to their children more than working-class parents do. The mother bathes her child in words, with running commentaries about the world, and about her own experiences and emotions, and with questions about the child's needs and interests. The working-class parent talks less to the child, and more of what is said is in the form of demands that would not likely stimulate the child's intellectual curiosity. The professional family includes the child in conversations at the dinner table, often attempting to engage the child in the issues that are being discussed, and exposing the child to vocabulary at the same time. Working-class parents in contrast are more likely to carry on discussions without any assumption that the child would have an interest in the topic or have anything to contribute.

The professional parent speaks about 2,000 words per hour to the child, whereas the working-class parent speaks about 1,300. By the age of three, the child in the professional family has heard about 30 million words, and the child in the working-class family has heard about 20 million. The resulting vocabulary differences are marked. By the age of three, the professional child has command of about 50 percent more words than does the working-class child.

Parents differ in how they deal with their children emotionally too, in ways that likely play a role in developing their intellectual interests and achievement. The professional parents made six encouraging comments to their children for every reprimand. The working-class parents gave only two encouraging comments per reprimand. Degree of encouragement by parents is associated with intellectual exploration and confidence on the part of the child—and the children of professional parents are way ahead of the game in this respect.

Middle-Class Parenting: Encouraging Analysis of the World

Much of what we know about social class and children's preparation for literacy and school life comes from the classic study of socialization by anthropologist Shirley Brice Heath. Heath spent many months in a town in North Carolina studying white middle-class families (all of whom had a teacher for a mother or a father), white working-class families (in most of which the father worked in the local textile mill), and black working-class families (who were mostly farm workers, mill workers, or welfare recipients). Heath literally lived with the families, observing them during all hours of the day and night and following the children to school. She found very large differences in the literacy-related activity of the three groups of children and in their preparation for elementary school. Heath's study was conducted in the late 1970s and her evidence base is just a small number of families in a particular community, but more recent studies, with a larger number and wider range of participants, found parenting practices differing across social classes in much the same way that Heath reported. In what follows, I rely primarily on Heath's work and the more recent work of Annette Lareau.

The middle-class parent reads to the child much more than does the working-class parent. There are lots of children's books in the middle-class home. Reading to the child begins as early as six months, as soon as the child can be propped up to look at a book. And the middle-class parent reads to the child not just as a form of entertainment but also to encourage connections between what appears on the page and what exists in the outside world. There is a deliberate effort to take what is read in books and relate it to objects and events in daily life and in the world. ("Billy has a black doggie. Who do you know who has a black doggie?" "That's a robin. Where did we read about robins? What do robins eat?"). Parents also encourage analysis of what is read ("What will happen next? What does she want to do? Why does she want to do that?").

From a very early age the middle-class child expects to be asked questions about books and knows how to answer them. Parents ask their children about the attributes of objects and teach them how to categorize objects based on their properties. (I once sat on a plane behind a father and his three-year-

Reported Milwaukee Activities Parents Perform to Make a School Choice by Income Group

Information–Gathering Activity	Low–Income (<$10,000)	Middle ($10,000–$30,000)	High–Income ($30,000–$50,000)
Visit School	76%	80%	92%
Child Visits School	71%	70%	82%
Talk to Teachers	76%	72%	87%
Talk to Principal/Administrators	64%	63%	82%
Talk to Parents/Other students	56%	54%	65%
Talk to Family/Friends	60%	64%	72%
Get Brochures/Printed Information	64%	75%	81%
Look at Web Site	18%	16%	32%
Use Parent Information Center	22%	13%	15%
Attend Meeting	36%	34%	42%

TAKEN FROM: Paul Teske, "The Information Gap?" *The Review of Policy Research*, September 2006.

old son. The father had a picture book and was asking the child whether particular objects were long or short. "No, Jason, pajamas are *long*.") Middle-class parents also ask *what* questions ("What's that?" "What did Bobby try to do?") and follow them with *why* questions ("Why did Bobby do that?"), and later with requests for evaluations ("Which soldier do you like better?" "Why do you like him better?"). Adults encourage their children to talk about what is in their books and even to tell stories that are inspired by the ones they have read.

Middle-class children are well prepared for school. They know how to take information from books, they expect to be entertained by them, and they are familiar with how to answer so-called known-answer questions—that is, questions whose answers are known to the questioner. The early grades go easily for such children. They are also more than ready for the later elementary years, when analysis and evaluation are called for.

Working-Class Parenting: Socialization for the Factory

The working-class baby is brought home to a house with some children's reading material—Little Golden Books and perhaps some Bible stories, maybe a dozen books all told. Walls are decorated with pictures depicting nursery rhymes, and there is probably a mobile. Family, friends, and neighbors talk to the child.

Although working-class children are asked questions about what is read to them, there is not much effort to connect what is on the page with the outside world. A book might have a picture of a duckling, and the mother might ask the child if he remembers the duck he saw at the lake, but then she might not explain the connection between the fuzzy yellow duckling on the page and the full-grown mallards at the lake. After about the age of three, children are not encouraged to carry on a dialogue with the reader. Instead they hear,

43

"Now you've got to learn to listen." The child is supposed to pay attention, and comments or questions are regarded as interruptions.

(A Philadelphia study illustrates both a symptom and a cause of the social-class difference in literacy. In areas where almost all adults are college-educated, booksellers had 1,300 children's books available per 100 children, whereas in blue-collar Irish and Eastern European neighborhoods only 30 children's books were available per 100 children. There could scarcely be a more stark set of figures capturing the social-class literacy gap.)

Activities in the middle-class family are guided by words. The middle-class father showing his child how to bat a baseball says, "Put your fingers on top of each other around the bottom of the bat; keep your thumb in this position here; don't hold it above this line; don't leave the bat on your shoulder—hold it above your shoulder a couple of inches." The working-class child gets no such elaborate instructions or experience in how to translate verbal instructions to physical practice. Instead the child is simply told, "Do it like this; no, like this." The middle-class family, when starting to play a new game, reads the instructions aloud and comments on them. The working-class family is more likely to guess at how to play the game and start playing it, making up rules as they go along. The middle-class mother works from a recipe, which she may read out loud so her child can make connections between what is read and what materials are being used and which procedures are being carried out. The working-class mother is less likely to use a recipe, and unlikely to give her child an opportunity to make connections between it and the materials at hand when she does use one.

Children and Class Differences: School Performance

Working-class children come to school with sufficient preparation to do reasonably well in the early years. They often know the alphabet; they can name colors and numbers and they can count; they can tell someone their address and their parents' names. They can sit still and listen to a story, and they know how to answer *what* questions about factual matters. But when they are asked, "What did you like about the story?" not many have ready answers. When asked, "What would you have done?" they are usually stumped. When categorization and analysis and evaluation are emphasized in the later elementary grades, such children are at a decided disadvantage. When they are asked to write a story, they are likely to merely repeat some story they have been read. When asked about counterfactuals—"What would have happened to Billy if he hadn't told the policemen what happened?"—they are at a loss.

Children who face these difficulties are likely to be demoralized and alienated by junior high school and are on their way toward being candidates for dropping out of high school.

The differences between the social classes that Heath found in socialization for literacy and school helps us to understand what happens to children's IQs [intelligence quotients] and academic skills over the summer, when they are not in school. The IQs and skills of middle-income children generally stagnate during this time. But there is a drop in skills for lower-SES children, whose families would not be expected to provide the degree of cultural stimulation over the summer that middle-class families do. The middle-class kids do not fall behind much during the summer because, undoubtedly, they engage in more educationally valuable activities, like reading and being read to, listening to stimulating conversation at the dinner table, going to museums and zoos, and taking classes in art, music, and even academic subjects. One study found that of children who are in transition between kindergarten and first grade, those in the highest quintile [one of five equal parts] of SES actually show an increase in skills over the sum-

> "More than 4 out of 5 parents . . . report that they did not lack 'any important information' when they made their choice."

Members of All Social Classes Have Equal Access to Educational Information

Paul Teske, Jody Fitzpatrick, and Gabriel Kaplan

Paul Teske is a professor and the director of the Center for Education Policy Analysis at the School of Public Affairs at the University of Colorado–Denver, where Jody Fitzpatrick is an associate professor and Gabriel Kaplan is an assistant professor. The following viewpoint examines the concern that low-income parents lack the resources to make informed choices about where to send their children for schooling. The viewpoint authors surveyed these parents, however, and found them satisfied with the school choices they made and the quality and quantity of information that led to their decisions.

Paul Teske, Jody Fitzpatrick, and Gabriel Kaplan, "'The Information Gap?': Academic Achievement," *Review of Policy Research*, vol. 23, September 2006, pp. 969–981. Copyright © 2006 Policy Studies Organization. Reproduced by permission.

As you read, consider the following questions:

1. Why did the viewpoint authors select Milwaukee, Wisconsin, and Washington, D.C., as the target cities for conducting a survey about school choice among low- to moderate-income families?

2. How does the level of satisfaction with their school choices of surveyed parents compare to the national average of parent satisfaction reported in the Phi Delta Kappa polls?

3. Among which group of parents do the viewpoint authors find a lack of information available or utilized about school choice?

M ost important [school] choice programs in the United States are aimed at low-income, urban minority families. Indeed, these are the choice programs that more Americans are comfortable supporting politically. In addition, middle- and upper-income Americans have long had a form of school choice, based upon residential choice options, that has not realistically been available to most lower income Americans, with their more limited residential options (which has been exacerbated, at least historically, by housing discrimination patterns).

Thus, low-income minority Americans have most often been "left behind" in urban school systems that have produced the least impressive test score, graduation, and employment rates in the country, and such students fare extremely poorly in comparison with students in many other nations. More choices are being made available to these students, but it seems likely that choice can only help if these families can make well-informed decisions. . . .

Surveying Parents About Their Choices

As part of the Doing [School] Choice Right project based at the Center on Reinventing Public Education at the University of Washington, we gathered new data on parent information. The purpose of the project is to better understand how low-income parents (and families) gather information, what they lack, who they trust as sources, and how such information might be better provided to them in the future.

We developed a new survey set of questions, using prior parent surveys as a foundation, but focusing more on the mechanics of gathering and using information, and less on the accuracy of that information. We implemented the survey in the late fall of 2005. We surveyed 300 parents each in Milwaukee, Wisconsin, and Washington, D.C. We chose Milwaukee because it has the longest history of vouchers and other forms of school choice, and choice is widespread and well established. We chose Washington, D.C., for similar reasons—more than 20% of D.C. children now attend charter schools and another 6 to 7% now attend private schools through both a privately funded scholarship program and a new federally funded voucher program. Indeed, D.C. and Milwaukee are probably the two large cities in America with the longest and widest school choice programs.

Our sample frame was aimed at parents of relatively low, or no more than moderate, incomes who have recently made a choice about their child's schooling. Since we did not survey parents who did not report that they "made a choice," even though all parents in these cities technically do have public school, charter school, and some private school choices to make, we cannot say that our findings are representative of all low-income parents, only those who report thinking about a school choice that they (correctly) believed they actually had. Still, over 70% of the parents who were called in these two cities said that they had "made a choice."

We limited family incomes to no more than $50,000. Overwhelmingly, our sample is female—about 90%. This occurs both because we asked for the main school decision maker in the family and because about two-thirds of our sample is single-mother households. The sample includes a near 50/50 mix of boys and girls, and a good spread across grade levels, but with more students at kindergarten and first grade; and fewer in high school, except ninth grade, probably because we asked for the "most recent" choice decision.

The city samples vary greatly in the racial makeup of the respondents—in Milwaukee, 54% are black, 33% are white, and 6% are Hispanic, while in D.C., 90% are black. Past evidence demonstrates that race can be an important factor associated with school choice.

Most of the students whose parents made a choice of which school to attend are still in public schools, including charter schools, while 26% in Milwaukee are in private schools, and 20% in D.C.

These parents report being very satisfied with their choice, which many surveys show for parents who choose, but parent satisfaction here is at even higher levels than most other studies. About two-thirds of these low-income parents report being "very" satisfied (at the extreme end of a 5-point scale), and nearly 90% are either "somewhat" or "very" satisfied. The annual, national Phi Delta Kappa polls, which include parents in all income groups, show only 70% selecting the top 2 points on their 5-point scale, where their scale asks parents to rate their own schools with a grade from A to E. It appears that our sample of parents is much more satisfied with their choice than national averages, even though we have a low-moderate income urban sample.

Most parents first became aware they had a choice to make through their social networks—21% in Milwaukee and 27% in D.C. learned from talking with friends or other parents, 20% in Milwaukee and 18% in D.C. learned from talking with teachers or school officials, and 14% in Milwaukee and 15% in D.C. learned from letters or written materials (like NCLB [No Child Left Behind]-issued letters). So, word of mouth is the central manner in which parents find out that they actually have a school choice to make.

These parents are willing to have their child travel to school. The majority are not sending their child to the closest, zoned public school. In Milwaukee, only 27% attend the closest, zoned public school (even though 60% of their parents did go to the closest public school, and 74% of students now attend some public school), and in D.C. only 44% attend the closest public school (again, even though 73% of their parents did so, and 80% are going to some public school). In terms of the perceived importance of a nearby location, only 8% in Milwaukee say location is "most important" (on a 5-point scale), while 29% say it is "not important at all." In D.C., 21% say location is "most important," while 27% say "not important at all."

Although this lower income segment of parents is viewed as likely to be less involved in school-related activities than higher income parents, most respondents actually report engaging in many different activities to gather information. . . .

In both cities, a majority of parents, often an overwhelming majority, engaged in most of these information-gathering activities, with the exceptions of using Web sites, school fairs, and information centers.

Lower Income Parents Feel Well Informed

Overall, we are surprised at the high information level that parents report in these surveys, which may be the single most interesting finding. More than 4 out of 5 parents (88% in Milwaukee and 82% in D.C.) report that they did not lack "any important information" when they made their choice. It could be true that parents "do not know what they do not know," but the high level of feeling well informed is supported by other data the parents provide.

A large majority of parents visited schools (often their children visited too), they talked to teachers and school officials, they talked with other parents and family and friends of theirs, and many also visited specific school choice events or programs. They also used written materials, like brochures and report cards, which they generally found readable and helpful, though more relied more heavily upon school visits and word of mouth than upon the written materials. Mostly, they did not utilize the Internet sites, supporting the notion that the digital divide is still an issue for these relatively low- and moderate-income parents. While we do not have more information about the quality of these contacts (e.g., "talking to a school official" could have been a hello in the hallway from the principal), these contacts clearly put parents in a position to get useful information.

While we do not have precisely parallel information from higher SES [socioeconomic status] parents, it is hard to imagine that their information-gathering activities greatly exceed the reports here. Indeed, there is little room for these percentages to go much higher in some categories. But, we can use our own sample to explore whether or not the higher income parents we surveyed (who should be characterized as "moderate income" when embedded in the larger American society) differ from the very lowest income parents. . . .

All income groups reported doing many things to seek information to make their school choice. Also, a majority of each group reports doing all factors listed except in the areas where no one does it frequently (such as visiting Web sites or going to an information center or meeting). But, our highest income group in Milwaukee is significantly more likely to visit a school, talk to teachers, talk to administrators, use brochures, and use a Web site. Indeed, the highest income group reports doing more of all of these activities than the lowest income group, except for using a parent information center.

When we examined the same questions for D.C. parents, we found significant differences for only two—higher income parents are more likely to have their child visit the schools and to use a Web site for information.

As previous research has established across the full income spectrum, our higher income Milwaukee and D.C. parents report talking to more people than those in the lower income groups—that is, they report having larger networks.

While a majority of all groups of parents say they are likely to trust information from other parents more than information from teachers and other school officials, by a 2 to 1 margin overall, the lowest income groups in both Milwaukee and D.C. are significantly more likely to have more relative trust in teachers. In Milwaukee, the lower income groups are also significantly more likely to say that a counselor would help them. Thus, the lower income groups seem to have relatively more trust in teachers and school officials than the higher income groups. Combined with the smaller network finding, it may be that these lower income parents recognize that their own friends and families may be relatively less reliable information resources than teachers. . . .

No Evidence for Significant Differences in Choice

Past research has shown that neither higher nor lower income parents have highly accurate information about the detailed elements of schools, but that, given choice, they can still often make a choice that works well for them. In our research, we focused upon the specific activities that lower income parents who make a choice actually utilize to gather information. Although we did not compare their responses directly to those of a higher income sample, we find that they report being remarkably satisfied, well informed, and active information seekers. Indeed, by looking at other studies, it seems that the differences between the low- and moderate-income parents in our sample group who made choices, and higher income American parents who have made choices, are probably not large. It is hard to imagine parents who report greater satisfaction, who are more likely to say they did not lack information, and who actually engaged in more information-gathering activities.

Our sample includes a wide range of income variation, from $0 to $50,000, which really ranges from poverty levels to moderate incomes in 2006 urban America. Within this sample, many elements of school choice information gathering and decision making also appear to be similar, regardless of the income and the race of the parent. However, when we examine the lowest income group in our sample, we do find a few important differences—though a majority report visiting schools and talking to teachers and administrators, they are less likely to do so than their higher income counterparts. They have smaller networks, they trust teachers relatively more as sources, they are more likely to choose a school close to home and/or with friends attending, and they are more concerned about school safety, relatively, and somewhat less concerned about academic quality. But, while these differences are important, we do not want to overstate them; even the lowest income parents report being very satisfied overall and being quite well informed about their choice. In addition, we find some significant differences by racial groups in Milwaukee, but they are not large either, and we find no racial differences on many issues.

All of this evidence suggests that there may be something of an income-based information gap in choice programs, but it is only at the very bottom of the income spectrum. Moderate and low-moderate income urban parents report behaviors very much like higher income parents on many information dimensions. This suggests that public policy aimed at overcoming information gaps should be targeted most prominently at the very lowest income groups, typically single-mother parents who are not employed. More outreach, providing multiple information sources, and parent information centers with counselors knowledgeable enough to advise such parents, seem to be potential solutions to help overcome this remaining information gap.

"*School districts that educate the greatest number of African American and Latino students receive less local and state money to educate them than the districts serving the fewest number of minority students.*"

The Achievement Gap in Mathematics Is Caused by a Lack of Resources

Alfinio Flores

Alfinio Flores is the Hollowell Professor of Mathematics Education in the Department of Mathematical Sciences at the University of Delaware. The following viewpoint analyzes the disparities in mathematics achievement between students from low- and high-income groups, and how those economic differences end up correlating with racial and ethnic differences. The author argues that the difference in funding available to teach students from poorer communities—evidenced by fewer dollars to spend on materials and less experienced teachers in their schools—is the primary cause of their lower scores on tests of mathematical skills and knowledge.

Alfinio Flores, "Examining Disparities in Mathematics Education: Achievement Gap or Opportunity Gap?" *The High School Journal*, vol. 91, October–November 2007, pp. 29–42. Copyright © 2007 by the University of North Carolina Press. Used by permission.

As you read, consider the following questions:

1. As explained by Flores, what is "out of field" teaching?

2. How do disparities in family income contribute to disparities in school funding in many public school districts, according to Flores?

3. According to the author, why hasn't it been clear that districts are underfunding their schools with high percentages of minority students and overfunding the schools with predominantly white student bodies?

By 8th grade, 91% of African American and 87% of Latino students are not proficient in mathematics, as measured by the National Assessment of Educational Progress (NAEP). This stands in stark contrast to the lower proportions of Asian American (53%) and white (63%) students who are not proficient. In fact, 12th-grade Latino and African American students perform as well as 8th-grade white students on NAEP's mathematics assessment. When assessing the depth of students' understanding of mathematics, the disparity is even greater than for multiple-choice items. For example, on the 2000 NAEP mathematics test the average score of African American 8th-grade students for multiple-choice items was 72% of the average score of European American students; for extended constructed-response tasks the average score of African American students was 32% of that of European American students.

This gap in mathematics performance has been very slow to close. Despite some narrowing of the gap in the 1970s and 1980s, since 1988 the gap has widened somewhat or remained about the same. There is also a considerable gap in test performance between students from poor families and those from non-poor families. Only 13% of students from poor families are at the proficient or advanced levels compared to 38% of students from non-poor families.

These data make clear that students from some groups are not learning as much in our schools as students from other groups. This can often lead people to jump to the conclusion that group characteristics are to blame. Researchers have studied several aspects outside the school system to try to explain the differences in school achievement among various populations, such as differences in intelligence, poverty and deprivation, cultural disadvantage and deprivation, cultural and language discontinuities, and the quality of the family's lifestyle. I argue, however, that it is important to analyze the practice and the structure of classrooms, schools, and districts to seek responses to two important questions: *Why do such disparities in school achievement exist?* and *What are the causes of these gaps?*

The Opportunity Gaps

Shifting the frame from looking at measures of educational outcomes to examining what students actually experience in schools results in a very different way of describing disparities among students in schools. This new frame calls attention to the fact that African American and Latino students are less likely than white students to have teachers who emphasize high-quality mathematics instruction, and appropriate use of resources. For example, African American and Latino students are less likely than white students to have access to:

- teachers who emphasize reasoning and non-routine problem solving;

- computers; and,

- teachers who use computers for simulations and applications.

The data that follow describe how African American and Latino students are less likely to have access to qualified and experienced teachers ... and are less likely to receive equitable per-student funding.

Access to Experienced and Qualified Teachers

Teacher quality, as measured by experience and qualifications, is inequitably distributed by ethnic groups and economic class. Classes in schools serving mostly African American and Latino students are twice as likely to be taught by inexperienced teachers (with three years of experience or less) as classes at schools where there is a majority of white students. Classes in high-poverty schools are also more likely to have inexperienced teachers. The percentage of inexperienced teachers in low-poverty schools is 11% whereas in high-poverty schools it is 20%.

Looking at teacher qualifications, the least prepared teacher recruits are disproportionately found in under-resourced, hard-to-staff schools serving predominantly low-income and minority students in central cities and poor rural areas. Thus, students who most need highly skilled teachers are least likely to have them, further magnifying inequalities. For example, in California, the percentage of under-prepared teachers in mathematics (who do not hold full credentials) rises as the percentage of minority students increases.

Out-of-field teaching—teachers who do not have at least a minor in the subject area they teach—has been a problem in mathematics for quite some time, and improvement has been slow. More classes in high-poverty schools are taught by out-of-field teachers (34%) than in low-poverty schools (19%). Classes in high schools and middle schools with high percentages of Latino and African American students are also more likely (29%) to be taught by teachers who lack even a minor in the subject area compared to schools with low percentages of minority students (21%). For core academic classes taught by of out-of-field teachers between 1994 and 2000, the percentages in low-poverty and low-minority schools remained essentially unchanged. However, there was a significant increase in the percentages of core academic classes taught by

Per Student Spending in Several Metropolitan Areas, 2002–2003

Metropolitan area	School district	Spending per student	% Hispanic + African American	% Low income
Chicago area	Highland Park and Deerfield (HS)	$17,291	10	8
	Chicago	$8,482	87	85
Philadelphia area	Lower Merion	$17,261	9	4
	Philadelphia	$9,299	79	71
Detroit area	Bloomfield Hills	$12,825	8	2
	Detroit	$9,576	95	59
Milwaukee area	Maple Dale–Indian Hill (K–8)	$13,955	20	7
	Milwaukee	$10,874	77	76
Boston area	Lincoln (K–8)	$12,775	19	11
	Lawrence	$7,904	86	69
New York City area	Manhasset	$22,311	9	5
	New York City	$11,627	72	83

TAKEN FROM: Alfinio Flores, "Examining Disparities in Mathematics Education: Table 1," *High School Journal*, October–November 2007.

out-of-field teachers, from 29.0% to 33.6% in high-poverty schools, and from 24.5% to 29.2% in high-minority schools. . . .

Opportunities to Receive Equitable Funding per Student

In many places in the United States, school funding is based mainly on local property taxes. Thus, schools in districts with a large number of well-to-do people have more funds per student than schools in districts with a large number of people in poverty. For example, the difference of per-student expenditure in the City of New York and other parts of the state was so big that the state was sued to allocate funds for students in more equitable ways. Recently the state's highest court ruled that New York City should be allocated at least $1.93 billion more per year. Although this is far less than the $4.7 billion set by a lower court, it is a clear indication that the funds allocated for students in the city were not sufficient.

Additionally, in many places a large proportion of African American and Latino students live in districts with less funding available. According to NAEP data from 2000, only 3% of white 8th graders are in schools where more than 75% of students qualify for free or reduced-price lunch, whereas 34% of African American and 34% of Latino 8th graders are in such schools. Conversely, a higher percentage of white 8th graders attend schools with less poverty. The majority of white 8th graders (64%) attend schools with less than one quarter of the students being eligible for free or reduced-price lunch, but only 15% of African American and 25% of Latino 8th graders do so. School districts that educate the greatest number of African American and Latino students receive less local and state money to educate them than the districts serving the fewest number of minority students. Students in schools with fewer resources are not always aware of how other schools provide better learning tools such as up-to-date books, science laboratories, materials for experiments, and access to technology within the classroom.

[Data] shows per-student spending for two districts in each of several metropolitan areas. For each district the percentage of students who are African American or Hispanic, and the percentage of low-income students is also provided. The pattern is unmistakable. In each metropolitan area, the higher the percentage of Latino and African American students, the lower the per-student spending. In some cases, the per-student spending in a low-minority district is twice as much as in the district with large numbers of African American or Latino students.

Often, schools with more low-income students and/or a large proportion of Latino or African American students have problems retaining highly qualified teachers. Teacher pay plays a role since districts with fewer financial resources are not able to compete with teachers' salaries in wealthier districts. Who would blame a teacher who needs to care for her or his family for moving to another school district where the pay is better? At the time the state of New York was sued over inequitable funding for education, the plaintiffs pointed out that the starting salary for New York City teachers was about 25% less than starting salaries in wealthy suburban counties.

Furthermore, the problem of unequal funding also exists *within* districts. Schools with a larger proportion of minority or low-income students within the same district often also receive less funding per student from the district in terms of teacher pay. For instance, in Baltimore City schools there are significant differences in the real costs of teachers' salaries between schools. While the district average was $47,178, in one school the average salary of the teachers was only $37,618, and at another school the average was more than $57,000. Thus, the teacher expenditure per student is very different from school to school. Consistently, high-poverty and low-performing schools are staffed with teachers whose salaries are lower than average. This happens because as more experienced teachers migrate from one school to another they take their higher salaries with them. More experienced teachers tend to migrate to schools with a larger proportion of European American students, less poverty, and better performance on state mandated tests. Schools with high needs are thus left with the least experienced and least paid teachers.

This example is not an isolated incident. In many urban districts there are huge differences in average salaries for teachers from one school to another. This inequity is not transparent due to the fact that urban districts calculate school budgets using average teacher costs. Thus, a school with a staff consisting of mainly senior teachers with higher salaries does not appear in the official budget as receiving more money than another school that is staffed mainly by beginning teachers with lower salaries. As a result, the fact that teacher expenditure per student is very different from school to school is effectively masked. Unfortunately, the schools that are shortchanged in this way typically have a large proportion of children in poverty and those that benefit from this budgeting system have a larger proportion of wealthier students. By using average costs for the school budgets, districts hide the fact that they are taking away from the poor to benefit the rich. For many years, federal programs that allocate funds that are meant to supplement and not supplant have ignored this practice. [Researchers] M. Roza and P.T. Hill point out, "Current Title I legislation allows districts to use average salary figures when comparing expenditures among schools. . . . Districts were henceforth allowed to maintain major inequities in school funding, as long as these were driven by teacher allocation."

By casting light on the inequities of opportunity faced by low-income and African American and Latino students—less access to experienced and well-qualified teachers, less access to high teacher expectations, and less per-student funding for their schools—the achievement gap is better understood as a manifestation of an underlying cause—the opportunity gap.

"Studying algebra in eighth grade yielded tangible benefits in terms of additional mathematics courses taken and subsequent college attendance."

The Achievement Gap in Mathematics Could Be Narrowed with Better Planning

Frances R. Spielhagen

Frances R. Spielhagen is an assistant professor of education at Mount Saint Mary College in Newburgh, New York, where she works with students who are training to become teachers. The following viewpoint examines the long-term academic benefits of taking algebra in eighth grade. Eighth-grade algebra enables students to more easily schedule twelfth-grade calculus, which increases their chances of college admission and better prepares them for college math courses. Spielhagen discovered, however, that minority students in eighth-grade algebra are significantly underrepresented and miss this college preparation opportunity before even starting high school.

Frances R. Spielhagen, "Closing the Achievement Gap in Math: The Long-Term Effects of Eighth-Grade Algebra," *Journal of Advanced Academics*, vol. 18, Fall 2006, pp. 34–59.

As you read, consider the following questions:

1. What was the difference in the representation of black students in eight-grade algebra and black students in the total population of the schools studied?

2. According to the author, what characteristic of studying mathematics puts students who do not take algebra until ninth grade at a disadvantage?

3. What evidence suggests that students of lower socioeconomic status are underrepresented in eighth-grade algebra courses, as cited by the author?

Educational policies have traditionally limited eighth-grade algebra to selected students who have demonstrated readiness or who have above-average mathematical ability. However, recent changes in curricular design and more stringent state standards have resulted in increased access to the study of algebra in eighth grade among larger populations. Standards-driven mathematics curricular reform has improved the skill-based infrastructure in the middle grades, opening eighth-grade algebra to more students. This development may bestow long-term benefits in terms of mathematics literacy and attainment among larger populations. The study of algebra acts as the gatekeeper to more advanced courses in both mathematics and science. Therefore, one hypothesis is that providing eighth-grade algebra to all students may enhance mathematics literacy across all populations.

This study examined the long-term effects of completing algebra in eighth grade in one large school district. The district had recently modified its long-standing mathematics curriculum to provide eighth-grade algebra classes for greater numbers of students throughout the district. The driving force for the curricular reform was the state mandate to raise proficiency levels among diverse populations. This type of mandate often results in districts devoting a large share of their limited resources to bringing students from basic to proficient levels on state accountability measures. The district in this study sought to raise proficiency levels among students by moving beyond basic proficiency and offering a course traditionally regarded as rigorous and appropriate only for students with the potential to study more advanced content.

This study first sought to determine the equity and the effects of the reform and then to explore the implications of the more inclusive policy. This study involved a longitudinal follow-up analysis of an original data set, which revealed benefits in the number and type of math courses studied after eighth grade. That original analysis also raised questions about the ways in which students gained entrance into eighth-grade algebra and the effects of eighth-grade algebra on future academic activity, specifically college attendance. . . .

The Promise of Algebra

Eighth-grade algebra provides both rigor and opportunity, while potentially enhancing mathematics literacy across the student population. If education policy makers consider early access to algebra as a means of increasing mathematics literacy, they must also provide equitable access to that literacy. Therefore, research must continue to inform policy makers of the benefits of early access to algebra, the availability of eighth-grade algebra to all students, and the implications of algebra study among diverse populations.

Several studies have chronicled the correlation between students' prior achievement, the timing of mathematics course-taking, and performance on state standardized tests. NAEP [National Assessment of Educational Progress] data show that students who study algebra in the eighth or even seventh grade do as well as or better on state standardized tests than their peers who have not studied algebra. Students who were studying pre-algebra performed better in 2000 than students taking the non-algebraic, eighth-grade math (270 versus 264 out of 500), and students taking first-year algebra do better than those taking pre-algebra (301 versus 270). Prior performance may have provided entry into algebra or even pre-algebra in eighth grade and may explain subsequent performance on state standardized tests.

Recent curricular reforms proposed by the NCTM [National Council of Teachers of Mathematics] address the potential efficacy of algebra for all students. However, the NCTM does not advocate the study of algebra in eighth grade by all students. The NCTM does emphasize the development and study of algebraic concepts starting in pre-kindergarten and continuing throughout elementary and secondary school. The incorporation of algebraic skills in the primary and intermediate grades may create a base for the study of algebra in eighth grade. The study of algebra enhances cognitive skills while serving as a gatekeeper to more advanced academic courses and enhanced opportunities after high school. [Researchers A.] Gamoran and [E.C.] Hannigan found that "whether cognitive differences among students lead to variation in learning rates, or not, taking algebra is still a good idea for everyone." Moreover, [Julia] Smith maintained that "the question of whether schools should provide advanced coursework to only a select few students remains at the center of this policy debate." [Maureen] Hallinan reported that her findings from a longitudinal study of high school students suggest that most students, with few exceptions, generally attain higher achievement in a higher level group.

Because algebra is the gatekeeper course to advanced study in both mathematics and science, offering algebra in eighth grade to all students can begin to address the decline of achievement in high schools in the United States. The sequential nature of mathematics precludes students from studying calculus in high school unless they study algebra in eighth grade. Students who wait until ninth grade to begin the study of algebra must double-up on mathematics courses if they want to take calculus in twelfth grade. Having studied calculus in high school, students are then better prepared for taking mathematics courses in college. Regardless of their long-term plans, students might well benefit from the nature of the content of more advanced mathematics courses in high school. . . .

Study Population and Research Results

These prior studies served as the rationale for an examination of one district's recent efforts to open the gates to advanced mathematics instruction to a greater portion of the student population while providing appropriate rigor for all students. To gain a baseline understanding of mathematic reform efforts at the ground level, this study addressed the problem of achievement gaps among underrepresented populations in a large school district in a southeastern state by examining the long-term effects of early access to the study of algebra. This countywide district borders a large southern city and has 36 elementary schools, 11 middle schools, and 11 high schools. The schools vary in diversity and socioeconomic composition across the district. Schools are located in varying neighborhoods, from urban-style enclaves to upper-middle-class housing developments to widely spaced homes and housing trailers in rural settings. Eighth-grade algebra was offered to selected students in each of the middle schools. In these eighth-grade algebra classes, all students used the same textbooks and followed the same curriculum and district-designed pacing guides.

Three research questions guided this research study. First, what was the demographic composition of the eighth-grade algebra class? Second, to what extent were the selection criteria for this course implemented in an equitable manner across all populations in the district? Finally, to what extent were there long-term advantages experienced by students who had studied algebra in eighth grade? . . .

College Attendance Among Students in Grade 8 Math Compared to Students in Grade 8 Algebra		
College Attendance	Grade 8 Math Total Group	Grade 8 Algebra Total Group
No College	31%	21%
2-Year College	23%	17%
4-Year College	46%	62%
TAKEN FROM: Frances Spielhagen, "Closing the Achievement Gap in Math: Table 8," *Journal of Advanced Academics*, Fall 2006.		

In the sample of students in this study, 45.6% (1,200) studied algebra in eighth grade, and 54.4% (1,434) studied it in ninth grade (the default option de facto not being selected for eighth-grade algebra). More girls than boys took eighth-grade algebra, both in the total population and in each ethnic group. Moreover, descriptive statistics further revealed that selection for eighth-grade algebra was disproportionate by ethnicity according to percentages of the two groups on the total population. Black students comprised 20% of the total population. However, they comprised less than 10% overall of the population in eighth-grade algebra and 30% of the total ninth-grade algebra population. Similarly disparate percentages were noted for females in this data set. . . .

Mathematics Courses in High School

When comparing the total student population, students who took eighth-grade algebra stayed in the mathematics pipeline longer and took more advanced mathematics courses than students who took eighth-grade math. The latter finding makes sense because of the sequential nature of mathematics courses. Without eighth-grade algebra, it is not likely that a student will study calculus in high school. However, there was substantial attrition in the number of mathematics courses students took after eighth grade. This, of course, can be attributed to many variables, including the varying aptitudes of students in the two treatment groups.

Participation in the early access eighth-grade algebra course led to further attainment in the quantity and quality of mathematics courses taken after the algebra experience. The state's minimum requirement for mathematics is two years of high school mathematics, including algebra. Most students followed the traditional sequence of algebra, geometry, and then Algebra 2. Students in the eighth-grade algebra class necessarily had a head start on this sequence. This early advantage affected the type of courses taken and the likelihood of taking additional mathematics courses, because they could ultimately advance to calculus in twelfth grade. Students who waited to study algebra in ninth grade often then took Algebra 2 as their final mathematics course in high school. . . .

The Long-Term Benefits of Eighth-Grade Algebra

This study examined the effects of increased access to eighth-grade algebra in terms of long-term achievement and attainment. This district did not provide algebra to all students in eighth grade, but instead opened the course to greater numbers of students in an attempt to increase mathematics literacy across diverse student populations, while maintaining a modified selection policy. In this study, restricting access to eighth-grade algebra made no significant difference in the outcome performance of the students on the state algebra tests, whereas studying algebra in eighth grade yielded tangible benefits in terms of additional mathematics courses taken and subsequent college attendance. . . .

When school districts address the needs of diverse populations, they must strive to maintain equitable delivery of services to all students regardless of their socioeconomic background. However, despite this district's intention of addressing potential inequity in curriculum delivery, logistic regression revealed significantly lower odds of being selected for eighth-grade algebra for black students. In addition, the distribution of students in eighth-grade algebra courses in the various schools in the district suggests a disparity of access to algebra in eighth grade according to the socioeconomic composition of each school. This was evidenced by the inverse proportion of students in eighth-grade algebra and students needing free and reduced lunch. This finding underscores the need for districts to be vigilant about administering more inclusive policies equitably across the total population.

Across the total population, the students who studied algebra in eighth grade ultimately took more mathematics courses in high school than those who waited until ninth grade to study algebra. This is an important finding that bears some examination and discussion. On the one hand, it is likely that students who took more mathematics courses simply had greater ability in math, greater natural interest in the subject, and greater satisfaction from taking math courses. On the other hand, a compelling question arises about the overlap group. Would the students in that group who did not study algebra in eighth grade have taken more mathematics courses if they had the opportunity to study eighth-grade algebra? Due to limits in data access related to student identification, subsequent math course taking specifically among the overlap group was not analyzed. However, because they had the same entrance credentials, having studied eighth-grade algebra might have opened the door to the possibility of taking more math courses in high school. The types and number of math courses taken in high school also relate to the sequential nature of the mathematics curriculum and state requirements for mathematics courses. Eighth-grade algebra provides an early start for taking more advanced courses.

Taking more mathematics courses in high school can contribute to the overall mathematics literacy of the students involved. In a study of six schools in New York state, [researchers J.] Spade, [L.] Columba, and [B.] Vanfossen found that "course taking is the most powerful factor affecting students' achievement that is under the school's control." Schools can address inequities related to social class by examining course offerings and the procedures used to place students in classes. Engagement in serious academic pursuits took precedence over demographic identifiers like race, class, and ethnicity.

Another indicator of attainment is college attendance. In the entire sample, as well as in the overlap group, students in the eighth-grade algebra group attended college at a greater rate than students in the comparison group. Does greater access to eighth-grade algebra increase college attendance among a larger base of students? These results support that conclusion; however, this study was descriptive and nonexperimental. Therefore, it is impossible to draw causal inferences from the results of this study. A variety of other factors (i.e., motivation, parental pressure, and the like) might impact both enrollment in eighth-grade algebra and subsequent college attendance.

Periodical Bibliography

The following articles have been selected to supplement the diverse views presented in this chapter.

Shaljan Areepattamannil and John G. Freeman	"Academic Achievement, Academic Self-Concept, and Academic Motivation of Immigrant Adolescents in the Greater Toronto Area Secondary Schools," *Journal of Advanced Academics*, Summer 2008.
Liz Bowie	"A Critical Gap," *Baltimore Sun*, September 23, 2007.
Dick M. Carpenter II and Al Ramirez	"More than One Gap: Dropout Rate Gaps Between and Among Black, Hispanic, and White Students," *Journal of Advanced Academics*, Fall 2007.
Donna Celano and Susan B. Neuman	"When Schools Close, the Knowledge Gap Grows," *Phi Delta Kappan*, December 2008.
June R. Chapin	"The Achievement Gap in Social Studies and Science Starts Early," *Social Studies*, November–December 2006.
Economist	"Nearer to Overcoming: Black America," May 10, 2008.
Alyssa McDonald	"The Pioneering Designer of the First Cheap Laptop for the Developing World, She Is Determined to Close the Digital Divide," *New Statesman*, May 4, 2009.
William H. Teale et al.	"Beginning Reading Instruction in Urban Schools: The Curriculum Gap Ensures a Continuing Achievement Gap," *Reading Teacher*, December 2007.

OPPOSING
VIEWPOINTS®
SERIES

How Do Schools Affect the Achievement Gap?

Chapter Preface

A very common lament about the American school system is that classrooms are overcrowded and teachers do not have enough time during the day to give students the personal attention required to identify and nurture their particular interests and talents, or help them catch up to their peers when they lag behind on knowledge or skill sets. In this scenario, struggling or uninterested students fall behind their peers year after year, and they gradually lose their ability to compete with their more motivated or better educated peers, first as students and then in the job market. In hopes of eliminating this gap before it opens up, many states have passed class-size legislation to give teachers more time to devote to every student. Class-size caps vary by states and grade level, ranging from a maximum of eighteen students in kindergarten to a maximum of thirty-five students in high school. Having fewer students in class enables teachers to better individualize instruction and communicate more frequently with counselors and parents to improve student learning.

Although data does seem to suggest that students perform better in smaller classes than in large ones, however, research does not support smaller class size as a solution to the achievement gap. Consider a 2008 paper published by Spyros Konstantopoulos in the *Elementary School Journal*. He investigated the findings of the four-year class-size study in Tennessee, Project STAR, and concluded that reduced class sizes do not reduce the achievement gap between low- and high-achieving students. In fact, he argues, smaller class sizes exacerbate it. Although individual student achievement increases when there are fewer students per class, it increases at different rates. Students who are already high achieving improve faster with personal attention than students who are lower achieving, at least at the elementary school level.

Results like these put schools and districts in a difficult position. On the one hand, if space and budgets allow small class sizes, adding teaching staff and reducing class size has the potential to improve the education of every single student at a school. Each student could learn more, do better, and anticipate greater success in adulthood. On the other hand, schools are not really judged on the achievements of individuals; they are judged on long-term statistics collected on groups and are frequently criticized when one group performs significantly better than another—even if all groups perform better than they used to perform.

Adjusting class size is just one proposed method of narrowing the achievement gap. The importance of the various methods schools employ to ensure every student reaches his or her potential cannot be overstated. The following chapter investigates some of the steps schools take to support the needs of high- and low-achieving students while attempting to mitigate the social, economic, and political inequalities of American society that follow students into the classroom.

> *"Academic stars like Pamela are generally smart and hard-working, but her success is also the product of her family's resources."*

Schools Reinforce Cultural Advantages

Jean Yonemura Wing

Jean Yonemura Wing is manager of Research and Best Practices for the New School Development Group of the Oakland Unified School District. The following viewpoint is excerpted from her book Unfinished Business: Closing the Racial Achievement Gap in Our Schools, *which she coedited with Pedro A. Noguera from New York University. The selection follows Pamela, a middle-class student at the racially diverse Berkeley High School, and shows how her family's college savvy and economic resources have helped her pursue an Advanced Placement curriculum and positioned her for certain college admission and probable graduation—personal advantages not every student has.*

As you read, consider the following questions:

1. According to the author, how do middle-class economic advantages benefit students in the academically rigorous Advanced Placement classes?

2. According to the viewpoint author, in what ways do the parents of high-achieving students use a school's systems to improve their children's chances of college admission?

3. What extra resources about college admissions do high-achieving students receive from their teachers that students in other classes may not get, as cited by the author?

Pamela is one of Berkeley High's academic stars. By her junior year, she was already thinking about which elite university she would attend. Her pathway to a highly selective college had been made possible by her hard work and commitment: She had taken several honors courses and consistently distinguished herself by earning high grades. There is no doubt that students like Pamela are deserving of the academic rewards they earn. Nevertheless, a closer look at her experience at Berkeley High School raises a question: How is it possible that she ended up "on a track with the same people"? That is, how is it possible that in a school as diverse as Berkeley High, a student like Pamela could find herself in multiple Advanced Placement (AP) classes and elective courses with a group of students who shared so much in common with respect to race, class, and social status?

Close examination of the processes used to sort students into academic tracks reveals that there is more going on than simply hard work and talent. Certainly academic stars like Pamela are generally smart and hard-working, but her success is also the product of her family's resources, of the reinforcement and encouragement she receives from her academically ambitious peers, and of her own ability to navigate a large, impersonal, and understaffed high school. Put more simply, the system at Berkeley High School works for students like Pamela. She enjoys several unacknowledged privileges, both inside and outside school, that allow her to "pick [her] classes selectively," tap into resources and social networks, and "really find [her] place" on the top rung of the high school academic ladder. With the backing and support she has received, there is little doubt that she will prevail in the fierce competition for admission to the most prestigious and selective colleges. . . .

"Capital Exchange" at Berkeley High

Economic, social, and cultural capital translate into privilege in the day-to-day interactions within school. The components of privilege in the context of Berkeley High School, like so many other aspects of the school, break down along racial lines. For white, middle-class students, privilege means having almost exclusive access to the most advanced classes and most qualified teachers, along with the academic support to succeed in these classes. It means being able to bend school rules regarding attendance, graduation requirements, and classroom behavior, with no negative consequences.

The various forms of capital also form a safety net for Berkeley High students in honors math. Although their ninth-grade math placement indicates that the high school considers them to be prepared for the rigors of honors math, in reality, many of these students struggle to pass. Parents of means hire private math tutors for their children, often continuing this practice throughout high school. The regional parent e-tree, a social network that has taken root primarily among upper-middle-class white families, abounds with requests from Berkeley High parents for advice on choosing the best math, science, foreign language, and writing tutors. Advertised at fifteen to ninety dollars an hour, private tutors are available only to those who can afford them (in other words, those with economic capital), and the utilization of the network and the information that is exchanged are examples of social and cultural capital, respectively. As one Berkeley High Diversity Project teacher commented,

> I never realized the extent of this phenomenon, but it is huge at BHS [Berkeley High School]. You have whole AP science classes supported by privately paid tutors. . . . It also means that an AP Chem[istry] teacher, for example, does not have responsibility to get the kids to really understand the material . . . because the tutors will actually teach it after school. Of course, the kid trying to get the education just from what is offered during the day is at a huge disadvantage.

Perhaps even more beneficial than advice about specific tutors is the information about the value of taking honors classes and Latin, or participating in crew or lacrosse, in positioning students for the fierce competition for admission to the Ivy League and other elite private colleges or to the most selective University of California (UC) campuses. This information is so well-known and widely disseminated among upper-middle-class, college-educated white parents that they consider it to be common knowledge—something "everyone" knows.

Navigational skills and knowledge cannot be underestimated in terms of gaining access to the most advanced academic classes. From 1996 to 2000, Berkeley High School's academic counselors each carried a student caseload of 550 to 650 students, which meant that each student, on average, could see a counselor (often a different one each time) for a few minutes a year. Students from affluent families have an advantage in this area as well. During the course of our research, we learned that a growing number of these students work with private coaches who assist them in writing college essays and packaging their applications to college. For students to enroll in the most advanced classes that are needed for admission to selective colleges and universities and to obtain their choice of specialized electives, they need navigational skills and some insider knowledge about how the system works—skills and knowledge that their counselors do not have time to provide. Moreover, one college adviser serves the entire student population of twenty-eight hundred to thirty-two hundred students.

Given this situation, middle-class parents play a role in counseling their children or in intervening on behalf of a child to gain access to certain classes or programs. Nicole, a class of 2000 white, female student from a nearby city, provides a description of how she, as an out-of-district student, gained admission to Berkeley High through the advantage of social and cultural capital and parental intervention. Nicole especially wanted to go to Berkeley High because, as she put it,

> [Berkeley High] has really high AP scores, generally. And other schools can't necessarily match, especially for a public school. And Del Norte High [the high school in her city] doesn't have the greatest reputation, and there were a lot of changes [under way at Del Norte], like they were going to go to block scheduling and all this weird stuff. And my mom's just like, "Let's forget it. Let's go to Berkeley High."

For this reason, Nicole applied for and received an inter-district transfer to BHS. Her permit was granted on the basis that she wanted to take Latin, which was not offered at Del Norte High. Nicole and her mother—like many other white, middle-class, out-of-district students and parents—knew that the best way to secure an interdistrict transfer was by requesting specific classes not offered in their own school district and which provide a bonus in college admissions. Nicole's "stay-at-home mom" also immediately sought ways to involve herself as a parent at Berkeley High and secured a parent seat on the influential School Site Council, which provided her with further access to other networks of middle-class parents.

	Berkeley High School Class of 2000: Family Income and 9th Grade GPA	
ZIP Code	Median Household Income	Mean GPA for 9th graders
94710	$22,866	2.19
94704	$17,930	2.44
94703	$24,499	2.46
94702	$25,389	2.49
94706	$34,522	3.02
94709	$27,105	3.17
94705	$46,689	3.25
94707	$62,567	3.30
94708	$68,911	3.37

TAKEN FROM: Jean Yonemura Wing, "Integration across Campus, Segregation across Classrooms," *Unfinished Business*, Jossey–Bass, 2006.

However, peer culture and informal student networks become the most useful form of social capital, as students make friends with those who are in the same classes and have similar interests, backgrounds, and aspirations. They share among each other which classes to take, which teachers to request, which counselor to see in order to more easily change their class schedules, which extracurriculars "look best" on college applications, and which classes to "waive" or take during summer school. Parents of high-achieving students frequently request waivers from classes such as ethnic studies and Social Living, which are one-semester, heterogeneous classes required for graduation. These parents seek waivers by citing objections to the content of the courses, particularly Social Living, which includes sex education. They do so for various reasons, primarily so that their children do not "waste their time" in heterogeneous classes and can instead take more advanced academic electives or pursue enrichment through the performing and visual arts electives—courses that "look better" on student transcripts for elite colleges.

Under these conditions, students' and parents' social and cultural capital, combined with economic resources, can make the difference between a good academic record and a stellar one. However, these kinds of resources remain unacknowledged and camouflaged for three reasons: (1) because they are part of the normalized and racialized landscape of success and failure, so that no one questions why so many white students are so successful; (2) because these nonmaterial resources are not readily visible; and (3) because they operate outside the formal structures and policies of the school. Thus, the high school keeps count of students who use the school-based tutorial and counseling services, yet private sources of assistance remain invisible. . . .

College Prep Courses and Unofficial Perks

Because the AP classes are supposed to be taught at a college level and prepare students for an AP test that will determine their college placement in a given subject area, Berkeley High first assigns the most subject-matter-qualified teachers to these classes. School and district administrators are well aware of Berkeley High's reputation for high scores on AP tests in every subject offered, and they are aware that AP classes play a major role in keeping white student enrollment high.

Pamela commented on teacher quality and remarked that she felt she learned the most in her AP classes

> because the teachers expect us to learn the most. Like, since they don't have low expectations for us, we kind of rise to the occasion. I think . . . you do struggle a little bit, but, like, especially in AP Chem . . . you have to do, like, twice as much work as a normal chemistry class because you're trying to get ready for the AP test in May, and it's supposed to be, um, like a college level. And you're reading from, like, a

college textbook and stuff.... So they also have good teachers in AP classes, but basically, they just give us a lot of work, and they usually are better at explaining things, and we have more tests, I think, than normal classes....

Berkeley High School has a single college adviser for the entire student body. She does an extraordinary job in providing information and assistance to students. She issues a daily bulletin with a calendar of college representatives who are visiting Berkeley High and other items regarding SAT [a standardized test for college admission] dates, scholarships, and other related information. However, in advanced classes with many seniors in them, teachers provided extra information to this top 10 to 20 percent of students.

On one shadow day in the winter of Pamela's senior year, several teachers gave out college-related information or made statements indicating their understanding that students faced looming application deadlines and that they needed to work on their applications and get letters of recommendation from other teachers. Pamela's AP calculus class teacher made announcements about a special state mathematics exam and provided some information for students who planned to be pre-med in college. In Pamela's physics class, the teacher announced deadlines for requesting transcripts from the registrar and for teacher recommendation letters, and underscored other college application deadlines. Students responded by stating that they were already aware of these deadlines and commented that UC applications do not require teacher letters. That the teacher made a point of reminding students, however, indicated that she saw these students as college bound and therefore focused on the admissions process....

Family Resources Confer an Exclusive Edge

Outside the context of Berkeley High, Pamela had access to a vast array of private college preparatory resources. She enrolled in private SAT preparatory classes in which she took numerous practice tests under timed conditions and learned test-taking strategies to maximize her score. She took the SAT once, but took the SAT IIs (subject area tests required by many colleges) multiple times. She reported, "I took math and writing. I took Math IIC [the more difficult test] twice, and I did really bad both times. So I took Math IC the third time. And I took writing three times. I took biology and chemistry too. I didn't take Latin."

Pamela knew from talking to friends and from her private college adviser that she could take the SAT II tests as many times as she wanted and put the scores on hold until she decided which three highest subject area scores to submit to the college admissions offices. Her parents hired a tutor to prepare for the SAT IIs. She also took a national Latin exam three times, stating that she did "pretty good. I got gold the first time and silver the second time."

When asked what her private college adviser did for her, Pamela said that the adviser first met with her during her sophomore year to get a sense of her personality and goals, then thought about which colleges might be most suitable for her. Her adviser kept her knowledge base up-to-date by visiting dozens of colleges a year and was in communication with many of the top colleges that are popular with local students. In Pamela's junior and senior years, her college adviser guided her through the SAT and admissions process, helped her with her college essays, and determined which would be her "stretch" school (where she was least likely to be accepted) and her "fallback" school (where she would definitely be accepted) and could attend if she were rejected by all other schools. . . .

In the end—through a combination of advice from her private college adviser, her SAT preparatory class, her ability to take the SAT II subject area tests several times and submit only her highest scores, and her overall high school record, complete with nine semesters of AP classes—Pamela was admitted to her stretch school, UCLA (University of California, Los Angeles). She commented that this made taking the AP science classes and advanced Latin—classes she disliked—well worth the sacrifice. She envisioned finishing college in four years, going on to graduate school, and becoming a successful child psychologist with her own practice.

VIEWPOINT

"Dropouts faced myriad institutional obstacles to building relationships with key gatekeepers and accumulating social capital toward achieving in school."

Schools Reinforce Cultural Disadvantages

Jamie Lew

Jamie Lew is an associate professor of sociology at Rutgers University in Newark, New Jersey, who researches the sociology of education, immigration and education, and race and ethnicity, especially school achievement and racial identities of children of immigrants. The following viewpoint is excerpted from her book Asian Americans in Class: Charting the Achievement Gap Among Korean American Youth. *It focuses on the institutional barriers that prevent students from poorer, less educated families and communities—who are already struggling in school—from achieving academic success. "Magnet High School" and "Youth Community Center" are pseudonyms for real organizations, to protect interviewees' privacy.*

Jamie Lew, *Asian Americans in Class: Charting the Achievement Gap Among Korean American Youth.* New York: Teachers College Press, 2006. Copyright © 2006 by Teachers College, Columbia University. All rights reserved. Reproduced by permission.

As you read, consider the following questions:

1. According to the author, what disadvantages do members of poor communities have to overcome to achieve economic success?

2. According to Theresa, a GED program administrator, why are so many counselors and teachers encouraging struggling students to take the GED test instead of staying in high school?

3. According to the author, what academic interventions have been shown by research to effectively assist students alienated by school culture?

While Korean American students at MH [Magnet High School] were embedded in supportive networks at home, in their communities, and at school composed of individuals who provided institutional support regarding schooling, the Korean American high school dropouts navigated through schooling alone, isolated and disconnected from institutional agents who could provide important schooling support. In contrast to the Korean American students at MH, who attended an academic school populated mostly by middle-class white and Asian students, the dropouts attended low-performing public high schools with academic standing below the city average, faced with limited resources, and populated mostly by low-income black, Hispanic, and Asian students. Consequently, the dropouts faced myriad institutional obstacles to building relationships with key gatekeepers and accumulating social capital toward achieving in school.

Poor communities are at a disadvantage in gaining access to and building social capital. The more affluent communities not only have greater financial and human capital resources, but they also have access to funded public institutions, like schools, that reproduce, if not advance, their economic position. On the other hand, the residents of poor communities may have strong networks within their neighborhoods, but those neighbors are not able to provide them with connections and references to high-paying jobs. Moreover, their public institutions, such as schools, are poorly funded and isolated. With these limited resources, they are more likely to focus on overcoming institutional obstacles rather than advancing economic and political opportunities.

Throughout the interviews, my informants spoke of attending high schools offering ineffective learning environments and few opportunities for constructing relationships with teachers and counselors who could help students with schooling. The Korean American high school dropouts explained repeatedly that even when they tried to learn in school, classes were often too loud and disorganized for any meaningful learning to take place. Robert, 17 at the time of this study and born in the United States, confided that because the school environment was not conducive to learning, leaving school would be a better use of his time and energy:

> I would go to the classes, but then my patience would run thin, and I would just get tired. Or I would go to class, but the kids are so rowdy that I can't learn, and the teacher won't teach. If I don't learn anything, there is no point of me being there. And I eventually just left. 'Cause if I came to school, I wanted to do something, not just sit there.

As earlier studies have shown, dropping out of school is but the final stage in a cumulative process of school disengagement, where students' educational engagement is associated with the extrinsic rewards of schoolwork as well as the intrinsic rewards associated with the curriculum and educational activities. Students' school membership is also associated with their commitment to and trust in the institution, belief in the legitimacy of schooling, and social ties to other students, teachers, and counselors who can guide them through schooling.

Given the limited structural resources available in these poorly funded and overcrowded urban schools, teachers and counselors also face tremendous obstacles in being able to provide schooling support for their students. The students I interviewed felt firsthand the effects of these structural problems in the educational system. In such school environments, students consistently mentioned the lack of academic rigor and limited academic and social support from teachers and counselors. Jung Suh, 18 at the time of the study and born in the United States, described his experience at a school characterized by low expectations and mutual disrespect between teachers and students:

> The thing about New York school, as to why I lost the passion to learn, or whatever, is because first of all, I don't like the teachers, how they treat you . . . I mean, a good teacher can make a bad subject worthwhile. And I came here, and it's not like that. They all think you are ignorant, and they talk to you like you are ignorant, and honestly, it just pisses me off. I didn't want to stay there, and personally, I don't like being looked down upon and seen as if I am stupid. And that's very offensive to me, so I just left. And it's not just seeing it happen to me, I don't like seeing it happen to others, too. . . .

Struggling Students Are Encouraged to Leave School

The overall poor relationships with teachers and counselors reiterated by my informants, however, cannot be understood adequately without examining the larger social forces that schools are subjected to. Schools are increasingly facing pressure from federal and state agencies to improve their performance, and assessment is based largely on standardized exams and graduation rates. When such mandates are handed down without providing adequate structural resources to meet these standards, there is less incentive to help the most needy students in the school system. Studies have shown that in the face of such testing and assessment policies, schools have resorted to "pushing out" students who are "at risk" in order to improve school performance. That is, the panoply of high-stakes testing could result in adverse outcomes, such as increase in rates of high school dropouts and "push-outs."

In line with this, numerous Korean American high school dropouts interviewed spoke of their receiving inadequate counseling, and some confided that they were advised to leave school and encouraged to take the GED [General Educational Development] exam instead. According to some of the students, counselors advised that they had a better chance of getting a high school diploma if they left school, given the students' lack of interest, excessive absences, low academic achievement, and likelihood of not graduating on time. What is notable, and unfortunate, in these cases is that students were neither adequately informed about the range of choices afforded them nor fully cognizant of how a GED might be different from a high school diploma. When I interviewed Hee Kyung, he was 18 years old and had dropped out of high school more than a year before. He explained:

> When I met my counselor, she said I should take the GED
> and not go back to school. I thought the GED and high
> school diploma were the same. I wanted to leave the school,
> and when I left, I felt better.

Like Hee Kyung, other Korean high school dropouts said they were encouraged to drop out of high school and/or take the GED, instead of receiving accurate information and the necessary resources to graduate from high school. Unfortunately, these systemic institutional problems caused many of the Korean American dropouts to see their counselor as authority figures who ultimately did not care about their welfare. These hostilities and disincentives to graduate—partly as the result of misinformation—left students feeling bereft of advisers who could guide them through a difficult process.

Consequently, the students exhibited anger, frustration, and mistrust toward their teachers and counselors. As Sam explained:

> The counselor was the one who kicked me out. First of all, I am not supposed to get kicked out . . . a couple of my friends got her for counseling, and she was really mean. All of them got kicked out. She will give me attitude. She'll say, "Oh, you again? Just leave the school." Just like that. That's why I decided to leave. I don't care.

Theresa, one of the program administrators of the GED program at YCC [Youth Community Center], confirmed this trend, for the organization had witnessed it throughout the New York City public schools. She explained that because the schools were crowded and under pressure to increase graduation rates and test scores, many teachers and counselors resorted to "pushing out" students who might need their support the most:

> It's easier for the school system to say to these kids, "Leave the school system, you'll be better off." Even though they are legally allowed to stay in school till they are 21, no one ever wants to stay in school till they are 21, and the schools don't encourage it because they are overcrowded, and the fewer students, the better for them. They want to keep that graduation rate high. It affects the test scores. It affects the way the school looks if they have students who are over the age of 18.

According to Mike, the program director of the GED program at YCC, these problems had become even more acute since the New York City schools implemented a requirement that all students take and pass Regents Exams in order to graduate. This standard has in some cases encouraged recent immigrant students with language barriers to drop out of high school and take the GED, all the while believing that this alternate route would be quicker and easier than enduring four years of high school. Implementation of these higher standards without adequate language assistance for recent immigrant children is one of the biggest challenges faced by some schools. Mike continued:

> You do have the more recent immigrants that do have serious language problems, and that's a big reason they drop out. And the Regents is a very, very big reason—an obstacle that most of them can't overcome. I don't know when, but year by year they added a new section and new test as requirements. You need to pass it. Now it's almost all subjects. So for a recent immigrant who came let's say two, three years ago that tried to pass a very difficult English test, they would realize that no matter how much I study, I am just not going to be able to pass this test. So they go, "Oh, I heard GED is easier, so I'll take it that way."

These comments from the Korean American high school dropouts have important implications for the rise in the number of students taking the GED in recent years. According to a recent report by the Urban Institute on the GED, there has been a steady increase of students opting to take the GED rather than graduate with a high school diploma. It is estimated that in 1967, approximately 150,000 people received a GED in the United States, but by 1998 this number had increased to almost 500,000, with about 200,000 of these recipients under the age of 20. The percent of GED recipients steadily rose from 2% in 1954 to over 14% by 1987. Moreover, an increasing number of GED recipients are as young as 16, further diverting teenagers away from obtaining a traditional high school diploma. However, there is ample evidence showing the labor-market costs of obtaining a GED instead of a high school diploma. That is, dropping out of high school to get a GED results in substantially lower income and earning later in life. Teenagers who are opting to take a GED instead of graduating from high school—as well as their parents—

How Did Educational Attainment Affect Personal Income in 2005?

Education Attained	Median Income	Average Income
No High School Diploma	$13,085	$17,299
High School Diploma/GED	$21,079	$26,933
Some College, No Degree	$23,153	$30,627
Associate's Degree	$30,937	$36,645
Bachelor's Degree	$40,166	$52,671
Master's Degree	$51,509	$66,754
Professional Degree	$76,497	$112,902
Doctoral Degree	$70,165	$91,370

TAKEN FROM: U.S. Census Bureau, "Income in 2005 by Educational Attainment of the Population 18 Years and Over, by Age, Sex, Race Alone, and Hispanic Origin," 2006. www.census.gov.

should be well informed of these findings *before* making the decision to drop out of high schools. . . .

The Link Between Ditching Class and Dropping Out

John dropped out of high school after having been in numerous schools for three years. He explained that, although he aspired to do well in school, after repeatedly cutting classes with his friends, he found it more difficult to go back to school:

> In the beginning, I enjoyed going to school. I am going to do well, this and that. But after a while, I cut a few days and then I wouldn't want to go back to school, and I would cut even more. And then when I go back, the teachers will be there, grill me this and that, or whatever. But then after that, I will keep going and then, I will lose the feel to go to school and' don't want to go anymore. You know, nothing was really holding me in school, and I lost the will to stay.

Students admitted that after missing so many days of school, it became difficult to go back to school and "catch up," which made it increasingly easier to drop out. As John explained, cutting classes gave him a chance to avoid some of the problems he was facing in school:

> You know, it's the simplest way to get a little bit. You cut school, and then you don't have to think about it. The school really doesn't care whether you go or not. I didn't care either. I thought, if I go to school, I will get into fights or made fun of, or didn't understand what they were doing, so why bother going to school? That's what I thought. And after you cut one month, you can't go back to school. You don't understand what they are talking about. If you want to catch up, you have to work really hard.

When I asked John if he had reached out to teachers or counselors at school for guidance, he reiterated the lack of caring relationships, mistrust, and overall isolation in navigating through the schooling system:

> I didn't have a relationship with teachers. I didn't really want their help and wanted to do it on my own. Guidance counselors tried to help, but I didn't like the way they did it. Like, once I didn't go to school for two months, and then I decided to go back to school. The guidance counselor called, and she kind of put me down and didn't encourage me. Like, she would say, if I kept this up I would get kicked out of school and not get a high school diploma. I don't really show them my feelings. I said, "OK."

The lack of caring relationships between counselors and students is clearly illustrated in the Korean students' schooling experiences. Researchers have shown the significance of caring teachers, counselors, and peers in schools, and how such relationships can initiate and build relationships that convey acceptance and confirmation of the students' investment in and contribution to the school community. For instance, [Angela] Valenzuela argued that the existence of caring teachers in the school community played an important role in Mexican American students' ability to build social capital in schools.

Students' comments also show that in the context of such limited resources at home and in schools, the students find it difficult to connect their academic aspirations and achievement. Providing students with institutional and social support, such as access to caring teachers and counselors, is pivotal for bridging this gap and achieving academic success. However, according to Korean dropouts in the study, they were not privy to such relationships. Given their school contexts, the Korean high school dropouts did not have access to important and caring relationships with teachers or counselors who might have been able to help them complete and excel in high school.

"The single most important factor in determining [student] achievement is not the color of their skin or where they come from. It's not who their parents are or how much money they have— it's who their teacher is."

Poor-Quality Educators Contribute to the Urban Achievement Gap

Joel I. Klein

Joel I. Klein is the chancellor of the New York City Department of Education, the largest public school system in the United States, serving more than 1.1 million students in more than 1,420 schools. The following viewpoint compares the effectiveness of general antipoverty measures to the effectiveness of better schools and well-trained, effective teachers for reducing the achievement gap between low-income and middle-class students. Although Klein concedes that better health care, housing vouchers, and parental support benefit students, he firmly states that improving the quality of teachers within classrooms, and thus the quality of schools, is the best solution.

Joel I. Klein, "Urban Schools Need Better Teachers, Not Excuses, to Close the Education Gap," *U.S. News & World Report*, May 4, 2009. Copyright © 2009 U.S. News & World Report, L.P. Reprinted with permission.

As you read, consider the following questions:

1. What argument about poverty and the achievement gap does the viewpoint author say is backward?

2. What evidence does the viewpoint author provide to support his claim that poverty is not the cause of low academic achievement?

3. What reasons do critics and skeptics of high-performing charter schools serving low-income students give for those schools' success?

No single impediment to closing the nation's shameful achievement gap looms larger than the culture of excuse that now permeates our schools. Too many educators today excuse teachers, principals, and school superintendents who fail to substantially raise the performance of low-income minority students by claiming that schools cannot really be held accountable for student achievement because disadvantaged students bear multiple burdens of poverty. The favored solution du jour to minority underachievement is to reduce the handicap of being poor by establishing full-service health clinics at schools, dispensing more housing vouchers, expanding preschool programs, and offering after-school services like mental health counseling for students and parents. America will never fix education until it first fixes poverty—or so the argument goes.

In fact, the skeptics of urban schools have got the diagnosis exactly backward. The truth is that America will never fix poverty until it fixes its urban schools.

Antipoverty programs are, of course, an essential part of bolstering our nation's low-income families. But to argue that these programs are the primary solution for improving student achievement is mistaken. Schools can and do make a critical difference, regardless of a child's socioeconomic status. Good teachers, effective principals, and great schools have a far greater impact on the achievement gap than any out-of-school antipoverty initiative.

Is it still an educational handicap to be raised by a single mom or grandmother on food stamps? Yes. An achievement gap shows up even before children start kindergarten—and we should implement effective antipoverty programs to help these families step up the economic ladder. Yet poverty can no longer be the default excuse for giving up on low-income minority students once they start school—and all the more so now that we have an African American president who was raised by his single mother and grandparents and whose family was forced to go on food stamps on several occasions.

Neither resources nor demography is destiny in the classroom—and no big-city school district demonstrates those truths more powerfully than the public schools in the nation's capital.

Low-Income Student Populations Achieve Differently by City

The claim that poverty trumps all in the classroom is belied by the fact that low-income black students in Washington, D.C., are academically behind low-income black students in other cities—in some cases, years behind. In 2007, the National Assessment of Educational Progress [NAEP], known as the nation's "report card," did a special assessment in 11 big cities. The NAEP results show that low-income black fourth graders in D.C. score about 20 points lower on the NAEP than low-income black fourth graders in Charlotte, N.C., and New York City in both math and reading. To translate that gap into plain English, 10 points on the NAEP scale is roughly equivalent to an extra year of schooling—which suggests that low-income black students in the District [Washington, D.C.] are two years behind their black peers in Charlotte and New York City by the time they reach fourth grade.

If the academic achievement of poor black students varies substantially from district to district, the mere fact of being black and poor cannot explain why low-income black students in Washington are years behind their peers in some big cities. By contrast, if extra spending and additional resources really were the antidote for the achievement gap, black students in D.C. should handily outstrip most of their urban peers. With the exception of the Boston school district, D.C. spent more per pupil than any other of the largest 100 school districts in the 2004–05 school year, according to a 2008 report from the National Center for Education Statistics. (Those spending numbers are not adjusted for local differences in the cost of living, but Washington clearly is a well-funded, big-city jurisdiction.)

It is true that no city has succeeded in eliminating the achievement gap between black and Hispanic students and white students. But a new generation of ambitious charter school networks that includes the KIPP [Knowledge Is Power Program] schools, Achievement First, and the Uncommon Schools has succeeded in raising achievement levels among low-income minority students to those of white middle-class students. These new high-performing schools, often called "no-excuses schools," demonstrate that effective principals and talented teachers can create a school culture of accountability to dramatically boost minority performance.

At KIPP DC: KEY [Knowledge Empowers You] Academy, fifth graders in the first class scored at the 21st percentile in reading and the 34th percentile in math on national standardized tests when they arrived. By the time they graduated from middle school in eighth grade, the students were at the 71st percentile in reading and the 92nd percentile in math, outperforming the average white student. Three of the four top-performing middle schools for low-income students in Washington on the city's math achievement test are now KIPP schools.

The Problem of Getting High-Performing Teachers to Low-Performing Schools

A major thrust of governmental policy has been to deal with the black-white achievement gap through improving the quality of elementary and secondary education for disadvantaged students. But, the actions taken have been unsuccessful in closing the black-white achievement gap, which grows across grades and grows most for the initially highest achieving blacks in Texas. The main results of this study suggest that the existing distribution of new teachers and the demographic composition inhibit black student progress, particularly high achievers in grade 3.

Because blacks are adversely affected by a higher likelihood of having new teachers and racial segregation, a redistribution of students that reduces the average share of blacks' schoolmates who are black and the probability of having a teacher with little or no prior experience would reduce the achievement differential, particularly for initially high achievers. . . .

Perhaps the most easily identified policies revolve around ensuring that black students do not draw a disproportionate share of beginning teachers, but the effects of any particular policy depend in large part on teacher reactions. Importantly, the underlying factors leading to teacher choices of schools are not completely understood, although there is evidence that a combination of locational preferences, working conditions, leadership qualities, and ease of the teaching challenges contribute.

> *Eric A. Hanushek and Steven G. Rivkin,*
> *"Harming the Best: How Schools Affect*
> *the Black-White Achievement Gap,"*
> Journal of Policy Analysis and Management, *Summer 2009.*

Debunking Criticisms of Low-Income, High-Performing

Yet the response to no-excuses schools has been to make excuses about why these gap-closing schools don't really matter. These high-performing schools succeed, skeptics contend, only because the schools "cream" off the best and brightest students or have exceptionally motivated two-parent families that push kids to succeed. The first in-depth examination of these inner-city secondary schools, David Whitman's recent book, *Sweating the Small Stuff[: Inner-City Schools and the New Paternalism]*, debunks these claims. He finds that students at no-excuses schools are typically one to two grade levels behind when they arrive and that they are not from two-parent superstriver families.

Still, in the absence of controlled experiments with random assignment of students, skeptics of high-performing schools could continue to maintain that an unknown demographic X factor explains their success—until now. A new study by Harvard Prof. Thomas Kane and a team of researchers for the Boston Foundation shows that popular charter schools in Boston do in fact rapidly narrow the achievement gap, even after taking account of the characteristics of the students attending the charters.

The Boston Foundation study compares the growth in academic achievement of students who won charter school lotteries and enrolled in charter schools with that of lottery losers who had to remain in traditional public schools in Boston. The results suggest that the freedom conferred on charters to hire teachers and principals and to shape school culture made a huge difference in subsequent student performance. The students stuck in traditional public schools did only marginally better than their peers, but students enrolled in charter schools saw their achievement shoot up, especially in math. In a single year in a charter middle school, minority students closed half of the black-white achievement gap in math. According to Kane, charter school eighth graders' math scores were "very close" to the scores of eighth graders in Brookline, a wealthy Boston suburb.

Effective Teachers Make the Biggest Difference

While a demanding school culture can powerfully advance minority learning, boosting the number of top-notch teachers in inner-city schools is also critical to closing the achievement gap. As President [Barack] Obama has stated, "The single most important factor in determining [student] achievement is not the color of their skin or where they come from. It's not who their parents are or how much money they have—it's who their teacher is." The impact of a bad teacher is hard to overcome by good parenting alone. One study of 9,400 math classrooms in Los Angeles in grades three through five projects that if low-income minority students could be assured of having teachers who fell in the top 25 percent of effective teachers four years in a row (in lieu of a subpar instructor), those students could close the achievement gap altogether.

School improvement may not be the only route to narrowing the achievement gap, but it is the royal road to success. Putting more resources into antipoverty initiatives with a demonstrable link to student achievement, like providing after-school tutoring and extended learning time or offering eye exams and free eyeglasses to needy students with vision problems, is a good idea. So, too, is expanding high-quality early childhood education programs, particularly as policy makers identify ways to duplicate the enduring learning gains achieved in a number of model preschool initiatives.

Still, once children reach school age, no antipoverty initiative has an impact on the achievement gap that even compares to the power of better schools. That does not mean that programs like housing vouchers or expanding the earned-income tax credit are not important or vital to reducing poverty among needy families. But the evidence shows that it is the good teacher who holds the most promise for significantly reducing the achievement gap.

More than a decade ago, education historian Diane Ravitch warned that "we must take care not to build into public policy a sense of resignation that children's socioeconomic status determines their destiny. Public policy must relentlessly seek to replicate schools that demonstrate the ability to educate children from impoverished backgrounds instead of perpetuating (and rewarding) those that use the pupil's circumstances as a rationale for failure."

Today, it is past time to heed that advice. To close the nation's insidious achievement gap, we must replace the culture of excuse in our schools with a culture of accountability that works relentlessly to provide high-needs students with effective teachers.

"When numbed, distracted and ex-
hausted students walk through the
schoolhouse door, experts say violence
claims yet another victim—learning."

School Violence Contributes to the Urban Achievement Gap

Steve Giegerich

Steve Giegerich is currently a business reporter for the St. Louis
Post-Dispatch *newspaper; he has worked in journalism for many
different media outlets and has taught classes at Rutgers University and the Columbia University Graduate School of Journalism. The following viewpoint describes the rampant violence witnessed by children—as victims and as observers—in many urban
school systems and its negative effect on academic achievement.
The author also describes some of the ways that mental health
and trauma intervention programs can help students manage
the stress of living amidst violence, enabling them to learn better.*

As you read, consider the following questions:

1. As cited by the author, what American cities have put into place programs to help children cope with the mental effects of violence?

2. How do the psychological effects of repeatedly witnessing violence impact a student's ability to learn as explained by the author?

3. According to the author, how will teaching children to cope with violence protect them against becoming violent aggressors in the future?

Stephen Ross listed the litany of crimes that have touched his life with the nonchalance of a kid reciting the names of favorite teachers.

A cousin slain last year [2007], the fatal stabbing of a stranger he witnessed in 2004, an uncle stabbed and injured, a friend's uncle murdered, the two incidents when he was personally assaulted, a brazen burglary at [his] family's former home where thieves pretty much grabbed everything that wasn't nailed down, including the refrigerator. Stephen (pronounced Stefan) paused upon finishing the list.

"I'm not going to lie," said the Roosevelt High School junior. "It makes you scared."

The toll that kind of fear exacts on youth is becoming increasingly evident as researchers draw a line between classroom performance and the trauma and violence encountered by urban students.

It's a correlation, the experts are discovering, that leads to underachievement if not outright academic failure in places such as St. Louis.

An Unacknowledged Detriment to Learning

Preliminary research from the University of Missouri–St. Louis, [UMSL] for example, suggests that more than two-thirds of the city's public school students may be suffering symptoms of trauma tied to violence.

Steven Friedman, the executive director of Cleveland's Mental Health Services calls the repercussions of violence on urban youth, "the mental health issue no one was addressing."

Cleveland, in fact, is among the cities seizing the initiative. Its "Children Who Witness Violence" program, shepherded by Friedman's agency, has been seeking to counter the effect violence has on urban youth. Los Angeles has similar projects, teaming schools and social services agencies.

Pia Escudero, the project coordinator for the Trauma Services Adaptation Center for Schools and Communities, an acclaimed intervention program serving the Los Angeles Unified School District, said cities ignore the link between violence and learning at their own peril.

"If we ignore it, (young people) will become hostile and succumb to violence," she said. "Our kids will not achieve if we don't do something about this."

Although some St. Louis agencies deal with the emotional aftermath of violence, the St. Louis public schools do not have specific programs to deal with the issue.

But a research study at UMSL intended to measure the breadth and impact violence has on the district's 28,000 students, may provide the impetus for the city, and the district, to move in that direction.

Too Numbed, Distracted, and Exhausted to Learn

The early returns on UMSL's research are disturbing, yet, given the city's reputation, not entirely surprising.

Of the 75 children interviewed so far, 20 percent said they'd witnessed a murder by the age of 12. Another 50 percent had observed physical assault and 25 percent had seen someone threatened by a firearm.

The upshot is that an estimated 70 percent of children attending the city schools have symptoms consistent with post-traumatic stress disorder. Another 50 percent suffer from depression and 70 percent reported problems sleeping.

The current research piggybacks a five-year study, completed in 2003, that tracked 430 St. Louis children. Those findings concluded that when children are witnesses to crime they suffer a host of problems, from a loss of self-confidence to a negative self-image.

"If you're dealing with that every day, it would get to the point where you're not feeling much," said Lois Pierce, the UMSL professor and head of the school's Sociology Department heading the research project.

Living in a neighborhood where she hears the sound of "gunshots all the time," Roosevelt High junior Lonnie Lesuer suppresses her feelings as a coping mechanism.

"Sleet, snow, rain, it doesn't matter. It's no telling, they just shoot a lot," she said. "You can push it aside, you've got to, you can't hold onto it for a long time."

When numbed, distracted and exhausted students walk through the schoolhouse door, experts say violence claims yet another victim—learning.

"It's part of the achievement gap," said Escudero, of the trauma program in Los Angeles. "And it's something we see here every day."

Spurred by findings similar to the St. Louis research, the Los Angeles program got its start 20 years ago with the support of schools, social service agencies, mental health organizations and the University of California, Los Angeles [UCLA].

The project now estimates that 99 percent of students in the Los Angeles system have been exposed to violence, 33 percent suffer from post-traumatic stress disorder and 16 percent are clinically depressed.

In response to those numbers, the center dispatches mental health workers, school counselors and, increasingly, teachers to assist students with the consequences of living where the sound of gunfire is ubiquitous.

"You can't just teach the counselors," said Escudero. "You need to teach the teachers, too, or it won't help."

Treating the Problem One Student at a Time

Cleveland's initiative began in 1997, when Mental Health Services joined with social services, law enforcement, the schools and Rainbow Babies and Children's Hospital to form the "Children Who Witness Violence" program.

Under the program, when children are exposed to domestic violence or the death or injury of a loved one, police summon an "EMS [emergency medical services] response for social services." If necessary, counselors assist the family with funeral arrangements, provide food and even advice on how to deal with the media.

From that point, the children are monitored and assessed. Schools are placed on alert. Within 90 days, a referral is usually made for long-term counseling. Approximately 40 percent of the families take advantage of the offer, said Rosemary Creeden, the program manager.

The program has been so successful at treating the "emotional consequences" of violence for immediate families that Creeden hopes to expand the service to children once, twice or more removed from violent acts.

"The model of our program is to recognize that the impact of these events extends through a whole network of people," she said.

Pierce, of UMSL, points out that ending the cycle that spirals from one act of violence into another should be the underlying objective of all counseling programs involving youths in violent urban environments.

Boys in particular identify with aggressors, she said, because "they believe that if you can be like the people you are afraid of, then you have less reason to be afraid."

Stephen Ross provided a textbook example of that reasoning.

"You can't let them know how scared you are," he said. "So you have to act manly around them. It's not making you masculine, it's making you as scared as they are."

The two assaults weighing heavy in his mind, Stephen says he has learned to protect himself.

That protection, he emphasized, does not involve weapons.

> *"Many young men tend to gravitate to-*
> *ward material that many teachers find*
> *unacceptable—comic books, books that*
> *are goofy and irreverent, and maga-*
> *zines."*

Boys Achieve Less in Literacy Because Schools Do Not Support Their Interests

Peg Tyre

Peg Tyre is an award-winning, investigative journalist who has written for magazines and newspapers and worked as an on-air correspondent for CNN. She specializes in the topics of education, social trends, and culture. The following viewpoint is excerpted from her book The Trouble with Boys: A Surprising Report Card on Our Sons, Their Problems at School, and What Parents and Educators Must Do, *an examination of the academic and social factors that might contribute to the disparity between male and female school achievement and college attendance. Tyre argues that girls outperform boys in reading and writing because elementary school teachers—who are mostly female—disapprove of and devalue boys' interests, thus unwittingly deflecting boys from literacy.*

As you read, consider the following questions:

1. As cited by Tyre, how do the literacy and writing skills of male high school seniors compare to the skills of their female classmates?

2. According to the viewpoint author, how has the act of reading become associated with feminine behaviors?

3. According to the teacher/author Jon Scieszka, what kinds of topics do boys like to read about?

In 1999, Dr. Gary Phillips, acting commissioner of the National Center for Education Statistics, released the 1998 *Nation's Report Card* on writing with this stark appraisal: "Girls had higher average scores than boys in all three grades tested and they outperformed boys in writing in every state and jurisdiction at the eighth-grade level. Girls did so much better in writing that, nationally, there were twice as many scoring in the proficient and advanced categories as boys. And twice as many boys were writing below the basic level at all three grades." Since then, boys' reading and writing scores have actually dropped, and some experts believe that a "male literacy gap" may be spawning a national crisis.

Boys' failure to keep pace in reading and writing is already echoing through our culture. In 2004, the National Endowment for the Arts issued a report based on data collected by the U.S. Census Bureau. Researchers found that between 1992 and 2002 young people of all races, incomes, and education levels were reading less. In overall book reading, young women slipped from 63 to 59 percent, and young men plummeted from 55 to 43 percent. The raw scores indicate that boys now do worse on national reading tests than boys did thirty years ago. Not reading, wrote the report coauthor, Mark Bauerlein, "is fast becoming a decided marker of gender identity: Girls read; boys don't."

We are failing to connect boys to reading and the repercussions are spreading like dry rot through our schools. Right now in this country, 33 percent of male high school seniors score "below basic" in national measures of reading achievement. The male literacy deficit does not solely affect poor boys, either—it affects boys from every walk of life. Psychology professor Judith Kleinfeld, who teaches at the University of Alaska in Fairbanks, runs a consortium called "The Boys Project." For a paper she delivered at the 2006 White House Conference on Helping America's Youth, she broke down the national achievement scores of twelfth-grade males and females by race and parental education. Among white high school seniors who have at least one parent who graduated from college, 23 percent of males and 7 percent of females scored "below basic" on reading. Six percent of white females with one parent who graduated from college scored "below basic" on writing; among males, one in four leaves high school lacking basic competency in writing.

In middle school, state test results tell us that the number of adolescent boys who struggle with literacy is shockingly high. In fifteen states, more than 30 percent of eighth-grade males scored "below basic" on state reading tests. In ten states, 40 percent of eighth-grade boys are barely literate. Those numbers surely include many rural and inner-city lads, but if you think the male literacy gap bedevils only poor boys, consider this: A consortium of administrators from the wealthiest school districts in the country found that the male literacy deficit is alive and well in plush communities such as Wilton, Connecticut; Ladue, Missouri; Oak Park, Illinois; and Austin, Texas. . . .

The Male Reading Deficit

We know that children who hear and speak plenty of words tend to learn to read more readily. We also know that in the home most little boys speak fewer words and get read to slightly less than girls. It would stand to reason, then, that kindergarten—which is designed to be a language-rich environment—would enable the boys to catch up. Kindergarten, however, seems to make things worse. In the fall term of kindergarten, girls outperform boys by 0.9 points in reading. By the spring semester, the difference has nearly doubled to 1.7 points.

Early in elementary school, classes divide—sometimes formally, sometimes informally—into good readers and not-so-good readers. Too often, the gap between them widens every year in what reading researchers call the "Matthew effect," after a New Testament parable about the rich getting richer and the poor getting poorer. In first grade, a child in the not-so-good reading group reads an average of 16 words in a week, and a skilled reader reads an average of 1,933 words. As any primary school teacher will tell you, the more kids read, the better they read. The inverse is also true. By the end of fifth grade, boys who are poor readers are at a disadvantage from which they will never recover. By middle school, a poor reader reads 100,000 words a year, an average reader 1 million words, and a voracious reader 10 million words.

Around fourth and fifth grade, another factor comes into play as well. Good readers take a leap forward as they move from learning to read to reading to learn. The curriculum demands it. It's no longer enough to be able to "sound out" words. Children have to comprehend sentences and paragraphs from history and science books and make inferences from those texts. Kids who don't make that jump fall into what experts have dubbed the "fourth-grade slump." They are stuck trying to figure out how to decode the word *everglades*, for instance, while other kids are learning about the kinds of animals that live in those Florida swamps. It's an important cognitive leap.

By every measure, the fourth-grade slump hits boys harder than it hits girls. This is reflected in boys' engagement in school and in reading. In 2006, Scholastic, a publisher of materials for children, commissioned one of the nation's top polling firms, Yankelovich, to do a study of the attitudes of nine-year-old boys and girls toward reading. Children were asked if they like to read. More girls than boys were reading enthusiasts (49 percent of boys, 57 percent of girls). More boys than girls said that they didn't like it (10 percent of boys answered "not at all," 6 percent of girls). Those little boys become what Thomas Newkirk, professor of English at the University of New Hampshire and author of the seminal book *Misreading Masculinity: Boys, Literacy, and Popular Culture*, calls "reluctant readers." "Boys don't like reading," he says, "so they don't read." It's a disastrous decision. When they turn off reading so young, says Newkirk, "they can't build up enough stamina to read in a sustained way."

The fourth-grade slump draws those boys inexorably toward the "eighth-grade cliff." Because girls read so much better than boys, struggling boy readers, perhaps defensively looking for reasons why they're not succeeding, begin to express the opinion that reading is "feminine." Then they go out of their way to avoid things that they classify as "girlie" activities. It's a silly, self-defeating pattern, but boys find plenty of support for this attitude in their families and their culture. Mom is the person who usually reads them a bedtime story. Mom is the person who makes up the grocery list or follows the recipe. Mom is the person who is most likely to buy books, read magazines, and take books out of the library. She's the person they're most likely to barge in on reading a novel.

What do boys conclude about the world of reading? Men don't read. So boys begin to check out, and the consequences are almost inevitable. . . .

Less Brontë, More Bond

Vivian Gussin Paley, who taught kindergarten and nursery school for thirty-seven years at the University of Chicago's renowned Laboratory School, is a keen and sensitive observer of classroom dynamics. In the 1984 book about early education *Boys and Girls: Superheroes in the Doll Corner*, Gussin Paley, who is the only early childhood teacher to win a MacArthur [Fellowship] award, contrasts the natural, unaffected ways in which little boys and little girls tell stories.

Here's the girls' story: "Once there were four kittens and they found a pretty bunny. Then they went to buy the bunny some food and they fed the baby bunny and then they went on a picnic."

Here's the boys' story: "We sneaked up in the house. Then we put the good guys in jail. Then we killed some of the good guys. Then the four bad guys got some money and some jewels."

"Kindergarten," Gussin Paley writes, "is a triumph of sexual stereotyping. No amount of adult subterfuge or propaganda deflects the five-year-olds' passion for segregation by sex. They think they have invented the difference between boys and girls and, as with any new invention, must prove that it works."

What is true of storytelling is also true of what kind of stories girls and boys like to read. All children use the same simple books to learn to read. Once they are fluent enough to take their first tentative steps toward independent reading, they are at an important crossroads: They need to read material that jibes with their natural penchant for telling stories. Unfortunately for our boys, many young men tend to gravitate toward material that many teachers find unacceptable— comic books, books that are goofy and irreverent, and maga-

What Boys Like to Write About

- aliens, monsters, horror stories

- hero stories (usually fantasy or war-related)

- war, violence, drugs

- "thug"/fighting/gun stories

- war and military situations that involve guns/ammo or equipment such as jets, planes, tanks, trucks

- accidents and injuries

- mistakenly hurting someone else

- something awful that has happened in their life

- teams, sports, and . . . confidence . . . from sports

- dislike for school and/or certain mean teachers . . .

- driving cars or snowmobiles, dirt bikes, four-wheelers

- video games, movies, cartoon-related stories . . .

- popular movie figures, typically action figures

- activity with their fathers: fishing, hunting, sports events

- toys and electronic games . . .

- fantasy worlds (often stems out of popular literature)

- rescue vehicles (helicopters and fire engines)

- robots, fighting and destroying evil characters, etc.

- computer/video games

Ralph Fletcher, Boy Writers: Reclaiming Their Voices.
Portland, ME: Stenhouse Publishers, 2006.

zines. And rather than encourage their attempts to tackle a new work of literature, their teachers often advise them to leave their copy of *Captain Underpants*, their latest installment of *Spider-Man*, or their new edition of *PC Gamer* at home.

What should teachers do instead? Jon Scieszka, elementary school teacher turned children's book author, is happy to tell you. In fact, he'd like to tell the whole world. An exuberant man with a shaved head and a wide smile, he has made it his mission to encourage primary school teachers to give boys the kinds of books they like.

"Boys," he says, "like books that are about stuff—science books about pyramids and grasshoppers. And books that are just facts, random facts, like the *Guinness Book of World Records*. They like books that have plenty of action. Books that are about men acting courageously in the face of danger. Or showing their loyalty. They like sports books and some biographies. Comic books. Graphic novels. They like funny books, too. Especially irreverent humor or books that mention bodily functions. Especially farting!"

He laughs out loud. Then he gets serious for a moment. "Not every book is right for reading out loud in class. I get that. But that's what boys like! We shouldn't make them wrong for liking to read what they like to read."

Why do boys like these kinds of books? Don't blame the parents. In this arena, nature wins out handily over nurture. In 2001, a Canadian researcher polled boys on their reading preferences, then investigated the children's families to see if there was a relationship between types of books and whether or not the child's parents expressed traditional ideas about gender. There wasn't a connection. Mormon families in Salt Lake City and lesbian couples in Cambridge, Massachusetts, are equally likely to produce a *Captain Underpants* fan. There's no link between how a boy is raised and the kind of books he likes.

Some teachers don't know how to handle it. Too often, writes English education researcher Elaine Millard, teachers of young boys "experience the change in boys' reading habits as a kind of denial of their own interests and values." It's an awkward moment when a teacher suggests *Little House in the Big Woods* by Laura Ingalls Wilder and her little male student opts instead for *The Day My Butt Went Psycho.* The latter choice can seem to signify the triumph of trash culture over literature or to exemplify the kind of loutish behavior that teachers know stands in opposition to good learning. So the teacher makes a face, in a chiding tone tells the boy, "That's at-home reading," and then helpfully suggests that he leave his book in his backpack, where he can retrieve it after school. Boys, forced to read a book they perceive to be "girlie" (girls love Laura Ingalls Wilder books for their attention to household details, their descriptions of relationships, and the challenges faced by individual characters and their families), make a decision. At what may be the most crucial turning point in their educational lives, they decide they don't like to read. And they won't do it.

I'm not suggesting that boys should get a dumbed-down literary curriculum—that little guys should read comic books while little girls slog through *Middlemarch,* or that a reading curriculum should begin and end with *The Gas We Pass: The Story of Farts.* Not every book should highlight bodily functions, and not every character should be a hyper-masculine sports figure, soldier, or secret agent. Let's not forget that one of the chief purposes of literature is to stretch your imagination beyond the limits of your own circumstances. And remember, too, that educated women have always had to bend their minds around über-male books such as *Moby Dick* and *Heart of Darkness,* which certainly weren't written with a female audience in mind. But reading experts believe that in these tender years of early schooling, teachers who champion the kind of books that girls like and ignore or marginalize the kind of reading that boys like may be hurting boys far more than they ever could realize.

Periodical Bibliography

The following articles have been selected to supplement the diverse views presented in this chapter.

Brent Champaco   "'Now I Like School': Educators in One Afflu-ent Suburb Shower Help on At-Risk Black Boys," *News Tribune* (Tacoma, WA), February 24, 2008.

Shirley Dang   "A Fine Line Between Inspiration and Segrega-tion: Racially Divided School Talks Reheat Fights over How to Close Achievement Gap," *Contra Costa Times* (Walnut Creek, CA), March 4, 2007.

Dana Goldstein   "Left Behind?" *American Prospect*, December 5, 2007.

Linda Jacobson   "Class-Size Reductions Seen of Limited Help on Achievement Gap; New Study Shows Great-est Value for High Achievers," *Education Week*, February 27, 2008.

Michelle Larocque   "Closing the Achievement Gap: The Experience of a Middle School," *Clearing House*, March–April 2007.

Rebecca Rosen Lum   "Study Ties Religion to Student Success," *Contra Costa Times*, May 28, 2007.

Don Martin et al.   "Increasing Prosocial Behavior and Academic Achievement Among Adolescent African American Males," *Adolescence*, Winter 2007.

Ann McClure   "Minding the Gap: Attendees of a Recent Sym-posium Explored How Community Colleges Are Addressing the Achievement Gap," *University Business*, July 2007.

Debra Viadero   "Black-White Achievement Gap Widens Faster for High Achievers," *Education Week*, April 16, 2008.

OPPOSING
VIEWPOINTS®
SERIES

CHAPTER 3

What Educational Strategies Narrow the Achievement Gap?

Chapter Preface

On October 21, 2009, the California Department of Education announced the launch of the "Signature Practices" online database, a resource for educators and policy members (and the general public) that allows them to search for the educational strategies and school climate changes that have led to improved student achievement and academic success. The information was submitted by the more than 250 secondary schools that had been awarded the status of "California Distinguished School" for increasing learning and closing the achievement gap. Signature Practices is part of the larger California government initiative to close the achievement gap between white students and students of other ethnic groups, between native English speakers and English language learners, and between students with or without disabilities. It is optimistic that schools struggling in these areas can learn from the case studies, interviews, and data from schools that have "beat the odds" and nurtured a student body that outperforms their peers in comparable settings.

The database will serve as a way for school leaders and educators to communicate how they have solved problems in their own institutions. California has nearly ten thousand schools in more than one thousand school districts spread out across 150,000 square miles; there is no way any educator or administrator could possibly know all the positive changes schools are making in the state, much less in the nation. A centralized location of success stories enables teachers and leaders facing similar problems to learn from each other, even if they never meet. It also puts information directly into the hands of interested parties, without the limited access of articles and reports that appear in subscription-only industry publications. Because California is such a large state with so many diverse school populations—from rural to urban and new immigrant to affluent—educators in other states will be able to find tools and practices for their own schools.

Not only does the Signature Practices database make available case studies of school success, it is compiled and maintained by dedicated educational researchers and analysts, who can assess the value of proposed strategies and help educators and administrators pinpoint why a particular technique was successful with a particular student audience. This partnership between school leadership and educational research helps to pinpoint what problems can be solved and how to improve learning for specific groups of learners.

Proven educational strategies can efficiently deliver useful information to students in ways that they can comprehend and internalize, which is important not just for the students' sake—public schools are funded by taxpayers, who want reassurance that their money is being used on programs that achieve results. Resources like California's Closing the Achievement Gap Initiative and its Signature Practices database help educators meet their obligations to the students who rely on them for instruction, and to the citizens who pay them for their efforts, by providing ideas, techniques, strategies, and materials that successful teachers have already discovered and adapted.

The following chapter analyzes the effectiveness of various educational strategies currently in use in attempts to reduce or eliminate the achievement gap, and explores how, and if, students benefit from such tactics.

"*Educational leadership promoting so-cial justice means providing all indi-viduals and groups in a society full and equal participation in meeting their needs.*"

Closing the Achievement Gap Requires Training School Leaders

José W. Lalas and Ronald D. Morgan

José W. Lalas serves as the director of the teacher education program and associate dean for the School of Education at the University of Redlands in California, where Ronald D. Morgan serves as the director of the masters program in school counseling. The following viewpoint explores the theories of educational leaders and discusses the concept of "social justice." The authors argue that promoting social justice within a classroom and at a school will equalize the achievement gap, because it will enable educators and students to see themselves and each other as individuals working toward a shared goal.

José W. Lalas and Ronald D. Morgan, "Training School Leaders Who Will Promote Educational Justice: What, Why, and How?" *Educational Leadership and Administration*, vol. 18, Fall 2008, pp. 21–34. Reproduced by permission.

As you read, consider the following questions:

1. According to the viewpoint authors, what is the benefit of educational leaders promoting social justice within their schools?

2. According to Marilyn Cochran-Smith, what skills do teachers and educators need to develop social justice within their classrooms and schools?

3. What are some of the criticisms Arthur Levine has made of Doctor of Education programs at many universities?

Closing the achievement gap between white, middle-class students and minority students who have a lower socio-economic status classification is a common outcry in education circles today. Indeed, recent studies document the assertion that students in urban public schools face many educational challenges and failures associated with race, ethnicity, poverty, and social inequality. [Richard] Rothstein explained that social class is a strong predictor of academic achievement in standardized measures and that school reforms alone such as higher standards, better teachers, more accountability, better discipline, and other educational best practices are not enough to narrow the academic gap between white, middle-class students and their minority and lower-class counterparts. [Pedro] Noguera characterized problems in education as a manifestation of social inequality rather than lack of technical capacity. He asserted that while we have the knowledge and resources to educate young people, the real question is "whether or not we care enough to provide all students, regardless of race and class, with a good education. So far the answer is no."

In *Divided We Fail: Issues of Equity in American Schools*, [Crystal] England discussed, with telling examples, the inequities plaguing the spectrum of issues that are essential to serving the needs of all students in our schools: inequity within diversity, inequity within assessment, inequity within standards, and inequity in curriculum. However, she also explained that "our situation is far from hopeless. ... There is time to act, a will to act, and a means to act. We have the resources to enact best practices, the technology to make our country more cohesive instead of more divisive, and the intelligence to engage in revolt, reform, and resolution." ...

Promoting Social Justice: A Vehicle for Educational Justice for All Children

We believe that what happens in the broader social community affects what happens in school. According to Noguera while testing, standards and accountability, and vouchers dominate current policy discussions, we neglect to consider the conditions under which students learn. He explained that simply listing schools by the percentage of students on free and reduced lunch provides us with knowledge about its potential academic rankings and the race and class makeup of the school. He also asserted that "we do provide all children with access to school in this country—public education remains the only social entitlement in this country—but we get unequal education."

Presumably, to many educators, promoting social justice in schools is a way of recognizing this inequality and respecting and valuing differences in race or ethnicity, cultural traditions and beliefs, social norms, intellectual flexibility, and personal perspectives among students in a usually multicultural classroom in urban schools. Classroom practitioners believe that social justice can be cultivated in students by recognizing and honoring diversity, appreciating equity, advancing critical thinking and openness, and encouraging individual voice and unique expression. Urban school counselors view an emphasis in social justice as an important skill in assuming an advocacy role as part of their work and paying attention to social, political, and economic realities of students and families. [Kathleen] Brown offered a practical, process-oriented model that is responsive to the challenges of preparing leaders committed to social justice and equity. She explained that being administrators and leaders for social justice needs grounding in learning theories, transformative pedagogy, and critical discourse and reflection, aims to perceive contradictions and to take action against the oppressive elements of reality, and prepares to "work with and guide others in translating their perspectives, perceptions, and goals into agendas for social change."

Whatever perspective is used in explaining the term, a strong argument needs to be made for "the necessity of a social justice agenda in a democratic and increasingly diverse society." Educational leadership for social justice is a set of beliefs that emphasizes equity, ethical values, justice, care, and respect. Others frame promoting social justice as a lifelong undertaking that involves understanding oneself in relation to others, examining how privilege or inequality affects one's own opportunities as well as those of different people, exploring varied experiences and how those inform a person's unique worldviews, perspectives, and opportunities, and evaluating how schools and classrooms can operate to value diverse human experiences and enable learning for all students.

[Linda] Darling-Hammond suggested in her definition that teachers for social justice need to understand one's identity, other people's background and their worldviews, and the sources of inequities and privileges. Sensitivity to these issues will be helpful for school leaders in facilitating the learning of students authentically in their schools and making a difference in the lives of teachers and students in the classroom.

[Lee Anne] Bell implied in a more philosophical sense that educational leadership promoting social justice means providing all individuals and groups in a society full and equal participation in meeting their needs. In her vision, a just society is where the "distribution of resources is equitable and all members are physically and psychologically safe and secure."

She further asserted that "social justice involves social actors who have a sense of their own agency as well as a sense of social responsibility toward and with others and the society as a whole."

It is clear from Bell's conceptualization that educational leaders who are committed to practice social justice need to understand that all individuals in the society must be responsible to each other and deserve to enjoy equity, security, safety, and involvement in their interaction and dealing with others and the society. Applied more narrowly to teaching, [Marilyn] Cochran-Smith framed promoting social justice in education as a conception of teaching and learning that includes the following instructional agenda: (a) learning to represent complex knowledge in accessible and culturally responsive ways, (b) learning to ask good questions, (c) using diversified forms of assessment to shape curriculum and instruction, (d) developing relationships with students that support and sustain learning, (e) working with—not against—parents and community members, (f) collaborating with other professionals, (g) interpreting multiple data sources in support of pupils' learning, (h) maintaining high academic standards for students of all abilities and backgrounds, (i) engaging in classroom inquiry in the service of pupil and teacher learning, and (j) joining with others in larger movements for educational and social equity.

In this description of the "social justice agenda" in teaching and learning, Cochran-Smith outlined the knowledge, skills, abilities, and disposition that teachers and educational leaders need to develop to move this agenda forward, which include culturally responsive teaching, making content comprehensible and accessible, effective and purposeful questioning, use of different forms assessment to inform instruction, support for students, collaboration with parents, community members, and other professionals, knowing how to interpret data, maintaining high academic standards, being a teacher-researcher, and strong advocacy for equity. She also implied that teaching from a social justice perspective is not a matter simply of transmitting knowledge and equating pupil learning to higher scores on high-stakes tests but rather engaging pupils in "developing critical habits of mind, understanding and sorting out multiple perspectives, and learning to participate in and contribute to a democratic society by developing both the skill and the inclination for civic engagement."

We view social justice as a vehicle for educational justice in K–12 educational settings. Educational leaders including school administrators, counselors, and teachers need to understand, value, and advocate for diversity and social justice because they are the foundations for providing ALL students with educationally just learning environments. . . .

Applauding Ed.D. Despite Arthur Levine's Report

During the time it took to create our doctoral program several questions and concerns surfaced regarding a doctorate program in education. From Arthur Levine's study came the suggestion to do away with the Ed.D. [Doctor of Education] degree. Levine concluded in his study that Ed.D. degrees are "watered-down doctorates" and have no future place in preparing educational leaders. This statement goes against the philosophy of what this degree is really intended for. His further statement about an Ed.D. degree being "unnecessary for any job in school administration" was both unfortunate and unfounded. To be leaders of school sites and certainly at the district levels requires a combination of theoretical understanding and practical experience. In the purest sense, that is exactly what the Ed.D. degree is designed to be—a practitioner's degree that consists of a blend of academics, scholarship and field experiences.

Levine's study also pointed out that "many university-based programs are engaged in a race to the bottom in which

"Nice Counselor Syndrome" (NCS) and School Change

It is challenging for many school counselors to avoid being drawn into NCS [Nice Counselor Syndrome] and to, instead, become effective multicultural/social justice advocates and organizational change agents. When counselors embrace these latter roles, they actively demonstrate their commitment to promote the right of all students to high-quality educational opportunities by confronting school policies and practices and challenging administrative decisions that reinforce rather than eliminate social/educational injustices.

Speaking directly with teachers who intentionally or unintentionally discriminate against students in marginalized and devalued groups or challenging administrators to address various forms of institutionalized educational inequities are daunting tasks to take on in the school setting. Undertaking such work is particularly difficult because it is likely to alienate and frustrate many persons who are content in maintaining the status quo. . . .

Counselors run the risk of being stigmatized as troublemakers when they are actively engaged in promoting multicultural/social justice advocacy and organizational change initiatives in educational settings. [Many] . . . may see such advocacy and organizational development efforts as being outside the expected professional role of school counselors, especially for nice counselors. School counselors who avoid expanding their roles to become multicultural/social justice advocates and organizational change agents increase their risk of becoming vulnerable to NCS.

Fred Bemak and Rita Chi-Ying Chung,
"New Professional Roles and
Advocacy Strategies for School Counselors,"
Journal of Counseling and Development, *Summer 2008.*

they compete for students by lowering standards and offering faster and less demanding degrees." If that is indeed the situation in some universities, then let us be proactive in reversing that trend and work on strengthening those degrees rather than eliminating them. In many universities, the Ed.D. degree is a rigorous program that combines a strong curriculum along with research expectations that most often require a doctoral dissertation. The candidates in many of these programs have a strong connection to local public schools and are taught the necessary elements to be a quality educational leader, which should be the goal of any or existing doctoral programs.

Unfortunately, some of the recommendations in Levine's study are the type of "knee-jerk" reactions that are often seen in the education arena. Rather than make the changes that can strengthen or improve an area that is lacking, recommendations are put forth that want everything thrown out and something new created in its place. The focus in this case should be to put energy into raising the bar on new and existing Ed.D. degrees in educational leadership—ones that reflect the important balance of theory and practice. . . .

The current research literature supports the creation of a program in educational leadership that has at its foundational core a strong emphasis in social justice. The Ed.D. program that we have created and continue to "massage" at the University of Redlands is a comprehensive one that provides rigor while balancing the theory and practice that is essential for today's educational leaders. Our definition of social justice comes from a variety of sources and implies that it is not only the development of our critical consciousness of the broader societal inequalities that are prevalent in our society, but also as a personal virtue of fairness, equity, care, respect, and compassion for all people regardless of race, gender, socioeconomic status, and other personal experiential backgrounds. Specifically applied to K–12 settings and classrooms, we argue

> "What you make of your education will decide nothing less than the future of this country."

Personal Responsibility Is Important for Academic Achievement

Barack Obama

In the following national address to America's schoolchildren, President Barack Obama urges kids to take personal responsibility for their education. While he acknowledges that many schoolchildren face challenges and obstacles, he urges kids to rise above those challenges to achieve academic success. President Obama makes the case that persevering in school is important not just for individual students, but for the success of the nation as a whole. Barack Obama is the forty-fourth president of the United States.

As you read, consider the following questions:

1. What careers does Obama specifically list that require an education?

2. According to Obama, is there ever an excuse for neglecting school?

Barack Obama, "Remarks by the President in a National Address to America's Schoolchildren," September 8, 2009. www.WhiteHouse.gov.

3. As described by Obama, what challenges did Jazmin Perez, Andoni Schultz, and Shantell Steve overcome?

I know that for many of you, today is the first day of school. And for those of you in kindergarten, or starting middle or high school, it's your first day in a new school, so it's understandable if you're a little nervous. I imagine there are some seniors out there who are feeling pretty good right now—with just one more year to go. And no matter what grade you're in, some of you are probably wishing it were still summer and you could've stayed in bed just a little bit longer this morning.

I know that feeling. When I was young, my family lived overseas. I lived in Indonesia for a few years. And my mother, she didn't have the money to send me where all the American kids went to school, but she thought it was important for me to keep up with an American education. So she decided to teach me extra lessons herself, Monday through Friday. But because she had to go to work, the only time she could do it was at 4:30 in the morning.

Now, as you might imagine, I wasn't too happy about getting up that early. And a lot of times, I'd fall asleep right there at the kitchen table. But whenever I'd complain, my mother would just give me one of those looks and she'd say, "This is no picnic for me either, buster."

So I know that some of you are still adjusting to being back at school. But I'm here today because I have something important to discuss with you. I'm here because I want to talk with you about your education and what's expected of all of you in this new school year.

Now, I've given a lot of speeches about education. And I've talked about responsibility a lot.

I've talked about teachers' responsibility for inspiring students and pushing you to learn.

I've talked about your parents' responsibility for making sure you stay on track, and you get your homework done, and don't spend every waking hour in front of the TV or with the Xbox.

I've talked a lot about your government's responsibility for setting high standards, and supporting teachers and principals, and turning around schools that aren't working, where students aren't getting the opportunities that they deserve.

But at the end of the day, we can have the most dedicated teachers, the most supportive parents, the best schools in the world—and none of it will make a difference, none of it will matter unless all of you fulfill your responsibilities, unless you show up to those schools, unless you pay attention to those teachers, unless you listen to your parents and grandparents and other adults and put in the hard work it takes to succeed. That's what I want to focus on today: the responsibility each of you has for your education.

I want to start with the responsibility you have to yourself. Every single one of you has something that you're good at. Every single one of you has something to offer. And you have a responsibility to yourself to discover what that is. That's the opportunity an education can provide.

Maybe you could be a great writer—maybe even good enough to write a book or articles in a newspaper—but you might not know it until you write that English paper—that English class paper that's assigned to you. Maybe you could be an innovator or an inventor—maybe even good enough to come up with the next iPhone or the new medicine or vaccine—but you might not know it until you do your project for your science class. Maybe you could be a mayor or a senator or a Supreme Court justice—but you might not know that until you join student government or the debate team.

And no matter what you want to do with your life, I guarantee that you'll need an education to do it. You want to be a doctor, or a teacher, or a police officer? You want to be a nurse or an architect, a lawyer or a member of our military? You're going to need a good education for every single one of those careers. You cannot drop out of school and just drop into a good job. You've got to train for it and work for it and learn for it.

And this isn't just important for your own life and your own future. What you make of your education will decide nothing less than the future of this country. The future of America depends on you. What you're learning in school today will determine whether we as a nation can meet our greatest challenges in the future.

You'll need the knowledge and problem-solving skills you learn in science and math to cure diseases like cancer and AIDS, and to develop new energy technologies and protect our environment. You'll need the insights and critical-thinking skills you gain in history and social studies to fight poverty and homelessness, crime and discrimination, and make our nation more fair and more free. You'll need the creativity and ingenuity you develop in all your classes to build new companies that will create new jobs and boost our economy.

We need every single one of you to develop your talents and your skills and your intellect so you can help us old folks solve our most difficult problems. If you don't do that—if you quit on school—you're not just quitting on yourself, you're quitting on your country.

Now, I know it's not always easy to do well in school. I know a lot of you have challenges in your lives right now that can make it hard to focus on your schoolwork.

I get it. I know what it's like. My father left my family when I was two years old, and I was raised by a single mom who had to work and who struggled at times to pay the bills and wasn't always able to give us the things that other kids had. There were times when I missed having a father in my life. There were times when I was lonely and I felt like I didn't fit in.

So I wasn't always as focused as I should have been on school, and I did some things I'm not proud of, and I got in more trouble than I should have. And my life could have easily taken a turn for the worse.

But I was—I was lucky. I got a lot of second chances, and I had the opportunity to go to college and law school and follow my dreams. My wife, our First Lady Michelle Obama, she has a similar story. Neither of her parents had gone to college, and they didn't have a lot of money. But they worked hard, and she worked hard, so that she could go to the best schools in this country.

Some of you might not have those advantages. Maybe you don't have adults in your life who give you the support that you need. Maybe someone in your family has lost their job and there's not enough money to go around. Maybe you live in a neighborhood where you don't feel safe, or have friends who are pressuring you to do things you know aren't right.

But at the end of the day, the circumstances of your life— what you look like, where you come from, how much money you have, what you've got going on at home—none of that is an excuse for neglecting your homework or having a bad attitude in school. That's no excuse for talking back to your teacher, or cutting class, or dropping out of school. There is no excuse for not trying.

Where you are right now doesn't have to determine where you'll end up. No one's written your destiny for you, because here in America, you write your own destiny. You make your own future.

That's what young people like you are doing every day, all across America.

Young people like Jazmin Perez, from Roma, Texas. Jazmin didn't speak English when she first started school. Neither of her parents had gone to college. But she worked hard, earned good grades, and got a scholarship to Brown University—is now in graduate school, studying public health, on her way to becoming Dr. Jazmin Perez.

I'm thinking about Andoni Schultz, from Los Altos, California, who's fought brain cancer since he was three. He's had to endure all sorts of treatments and surgeries, one of which affected his memory, so it took him much longer—hundreds of extra hours—to do his schoolwork. But he never fell behind. He's headed to college this fall.

And then there's Shantell Steve, from my hometown of Chicago, Illinois. Even when bouncing from foster home to foster home in the toughest neighborhoods in the city, she managed to get a job at a local health care center, start a program to keep young people out of gangs, and she's on track to graduate high school with honors and go on to college.

And Jazmin, Andoni, and Shantell aren't any different from any of you. They face challenges in their lives just like you do. In some cases they've got it a lot worse off than many of you. But they refused to give up. They chose to take responsibility for their lives, for their education, and set goals for themselves. And I expect all of you to do the same.

That's why today I'm calling on each of you to set your own goals for your education—and do everything you can to meet them. Your goal can be something as simple as doing all your homework, paying attention in class, or spending some time each day reading a book. Maybe you'll decide to get involved in an extracurricular activity, or volunteer in your community. Maybe you'll decide to stand up for kids who are being teased or bullied because of who they are or how they look, because you believe, like I do, that all young people deserve a safe environment to study and learn. Maybe you'll decide to take better care of yourself so you can be more ready to learn. And along those lines, by the way, I hope all of you are washing your hands a lot, and that you stay home from school when you don't feel well, so we can keep people from getting the flu this fall and winter.

But whatever you resolve to do, I want you to commit to it. I want you to really work at it.

I know that sometimes you get that sense from TV that you can be rich and successful without any hard work—that your ticket to success is through rapping or basketball or being a reality TV star. Chances are you're not going to be any of those things.

The truth is, being successful is hard. You won't love every subject that you study. You won't click with every teacher that you have. Not every homework assignment will seem completely relevant to your life right at this minute. And you won't necessarily succeed at everything the first time you try.

That's okay. Some of the most successful people in the world are the ones who've had the most failures. J.K. Rowling—who wrote *Harry Potter*—her first *Harry Potter* book was rejected 12 times before it was finally published. Michael Jordan was cut from his high school basketball team. He lost hundreds of games and missed thousands of shots during his career. But he once said, "I have failed over and over and over again in my life. And that's why I succeed."

These people succeeded because they understood that you can't let your failures define you—you have to let your failures teach you. You have to let them show you what to do differently the next time. So if you get into trouble, that doesn't mean you're a troublemaker, it means you need to try harder to act right. If you get a bad grade, that doesn't mean you're stupid, it just means you need to spend more time studying.

No one's born being good at all things. You become good at things through hard work. You're not a varsity athlete the first time you play a new sport. You don't hit every note the first time you sing a song. You've got to practice. The same principle applies to your schoolwork. You might have to do a math problem a few times before you get it right. You might have to read something a few times before you understand it. You definitely have to do a few drafts of a paper before it's good enough to hand in.

Don't be afraid to ask questions. Don't be afraid to ask for help when you need it. I do that every day. Asking for help isn't a sign of weakness, it's a sign of strength because it shows you have the courage to admit when you don't know something, and that then allows you to learn something new. So find an adult that you trust—a parent, a grandparent or teacher, a coach or a counselor—and ask them to help you stay on track to meet your goals.

And even when you're struggling, even when you're discouraged, and you feel like other people have given up on you, don't ever give up on yourself, because when you give up on yourself, you give up on your country.

The story of America isn't about people who quit when things got tough. It's about people who kept going, who tried harder, who loved their country too much to do anything less than their best.

It's the story of students who sat where you sit 250 years ago, and went on to wage a revolution and they founded this nation. Young people. Students who sat where you sit 75 years ago who overcame a depression and won a world war; who fought for civil rights and put a man on the moon. Students who sat where you sit 20 years ago who founded Google and Twitter and Facebook and changed the way we communicate with each other.

So today, I want to ask all of you, what's your contribution going to be? What problems are you going to solve? What discoveries will you make? What will a president who comes here in 20 or 50 or 100 years say about what all of you did for this country?

Now, your families, your teachers, and I are doing everything we can to make sure you have the education you need to answer these questions. I'm working hard to fix up your classrooms and get you the books and the equipment and the computers you need to learn. But you've got to do your part, too. So I expect all of you to get serious this year. I expect you to put your best effort into everything you do. I expect great things from each of you. So don't let us down. Don't let your family down or your country down. Most of all, don't let yourself down. Make us all proud.

"The EAAG [entry-age achievement gap] is largely an artifact of natural differences in skill between older and younger students."

Age at Kindergarten Entry Affects Future Disparities in Student Achievement

Elizabeth Cascio

Elizabeth Cascio is an assistant professor of economics at Dartmouth College in New Hampshire and was a visiting scholar at the Federal Reserve Bank of San Francisco (FRBSF). The following viewpoint appeared in the FRBSF Economic Letter. *It explores how the age at kindergarten enrollment might affect the achievement gap and examines research that suggests older, more mature children have better developed mental and physical skills, thus an advantage over significantly younger classmates. The author also observes that older students are eligible to drop out sooner and enter the workforce older, which could affect job earnings before retirement.*

Elizabeth Cascio, "How and Why Does Age at Kindergarten Entry Matter?" FRBSF Economic Letter, August 8, 2008. Copyright © 2008 Federal Reserve Bank of San Francisco. The opinions expressed in this article do not necessarily reflect the views of the management of the Federal Reserve Bank of San Francisco, or the Board of Governors of the Federal Reserve System. Reproduced by permission.

144

As you read, consider the following questions:

1. According to the viewpoint author, how is the hypothetical advantage of starting kindergarten older in relation to a student's peers a self-reinforcing benefit?

2. In what way does the viewpoint author suggest that a student starting kindergarten relatively younger than classmates will be put at a disadvantage?

3. In what way does starting kindergarten a year later add risk to a student's high school and adult career?

Those who have spent time in a kindergarten classroom know that there are remarkable differences in children's skills. Research has shown that these skill differences are strongly tied to age, with students who enter kindergarten later in life doing better than younger entrants. Moreover, an "entry-age achievement gap" (hereafter, the EAAG) has been found to persist until as late as the eighth or ninth grade.

Does this finding imply that parents or policy makers should push children to start kindergarten at a later age? The answer depends in part on what is driving the EAAG. In this *Economic Letter*, I describe possible interpretations of the EAAG, along with their implications, and discuss new empirical research attempting to establish their relative importance.

Three Interpretations of the Entry-Age Achievement Gap

There are three broad, and not mutually exclusive, interpretations of the EAAG. The first is "relative age"—that is, older kindergartners stand to gain over the long term because they are temporarily bigger and smarter *in relation to* their classmates. This can matter for school achievement because elementary school children are sorted into reading and other curricular groups on the basis of achievement, which, as mentioned above, is strongly correlated with age at this point in the life cycle. Placement in the top group can be self-reinforcing, since top groups may tackle more advanced material and move more quickly through a given curriculum. At the same time, older school entrants might become relatively more motivated for school or self-confident because of their relative standing in the class. Anecdotally, this concern has created an unsustainable race in some communities to secure one's own child the position at the top of the class, with "kindergartners pushing [age] seven."

Importantly, in each case, the result is "zero-sum": when older students gain, younger students lose, becoming less engaged with school, being placed in lower reading groups, etc. Therefore, a policy intervention that moves the date by which starting kindergartners should be aged five from December 2 (as is currently the regulation in California) to September 1 would affect who is at the top of the class and who is at the bottom, but not academic outcomes on average.

The second interpretation, "age at entry," is that older school entrants outperform younger school entrants because they are better equipped to succeed in school. While this interpretation of the EAAG might seem quite similar to the relative age interpretation, it differs in a very important way: Here, it is no longer the case that older students gain at the expense of younger students; rather, older students gain without affecting younger students at all. This suggests that increasing the minimum age at school entry may indeed raise academic outcomes of a cohort on average by promoting the achievement of students who would have otherwise started one year younger. Parents might also be able to improve a child's achievement by holding him back, giving him an extra year of preparation for kindergarten through more preschool and other enriching activities. However, any given child's achievement will not be compromised by other parents making the same choice.

The third interpretation, "age at test," is that age at school entry has no impact on achievement per se, but is correlated with cognitive development and the stock of skills that a child has accumulated outside of school. At any point after kindergarten entry, older children have lived longer and experienced more—had more books read to them by parents, taken more trips to the museum or the zoo, and potentially spent more time in preschool—than younger children who started kindergarten with them. The additional life experience of older students will eventually be minuscule compared to the stock of skills accumulated by their younger counterparts. If "age at test" is driving the EAAG, concern over age at school entry must rest on different grounds.

A New Generation of Research

Most empirical research on the EAAG has estimated the net effect of being older at school entry and has thus failed to separate out the individual contributions of relative age, age at school entry, and age at test to achievement. The difficulty has arisen because of a lack of data as well as a lack of independent variation in the three variables. For example, it is only possible to estimate the effect of age at school entry separately from that of age at test (holding time spent in school constant) if children who entered school at the same age were tested at different ages in the same grade, or vice versa, which is generally not the case. The survey data that form the backbone of this literature also generally lack information on respondents' peer groups, making it impossible to establish a child's age relative to his peers.

In recent research, [researchers Elizabeth] Cascio and [Diane Whitmore] Schanzenbach (hereafter CS) attempt to address the second of these challenges using data from a social experiment called Project STAR (Student Teacher Achievement Ratio), the original purpose of which was to estimate the effects of class size on achievement. In the fall of 1985, ap-

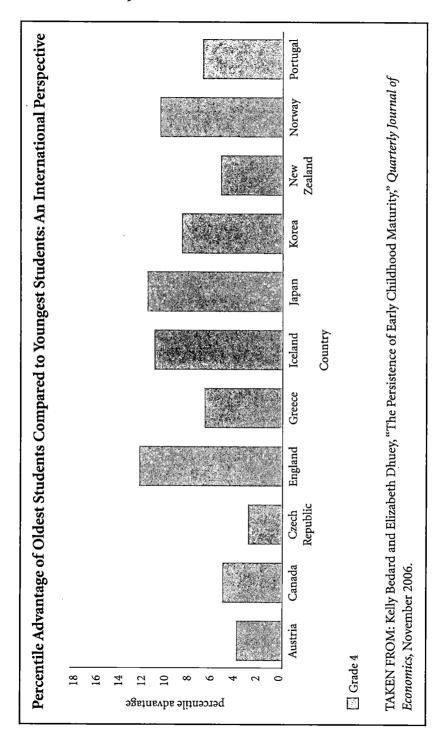

Percentile Advantage of Oldest Students Compared to Youngest Students: An International Perspective

TAKEN FROM: Kelly Bedard and Elizabeth Dhuey, "The Persistence of Early Childhood Maturity," *Quarterly Journal of Economics*, November 2006.

proximately 6,000 kindergartners and 330 teachers in 79 Tennessee schools were assigned by lottery to one of three types of classes—small (with target enrollment of 13–17 students), regular (with target enrollment of 22–25 students), and regular with a full-time teacher's aide. Data from the study are available on the classrooms to which each child was assigned and on test scores through the eighth grade.

The design of Project STAR thus allows CS to observe children who entered school at the same biological age but were different ages relative to their kindergarten classmates. Moreover, classmates were in general not chosen by principals or by parents, but rather were assigned to each child randomly. As a result, relative age should not be related to other correlates of achievement the researchers cannot observe or control for. To confront the additional challenge that parents exercised some choice over when their children started kindergarten, so that individuals who were older at kindergarten entry might have differed in other important ways from individuals who were younger, CS follow the common practice of predicting a child's age at the start of school with the age he *should* have been, given his birthday, if his parents had complied with local school-entry regulations. School entry ages of a child's peers, and hence his relative age, are predicted in the same way.

Their findings suggest that relative age does not explain the EAAG. In fact, CS find that children assigned to classrooms where the gap between their own age and the age of their peers on average—one possible measure of relative maturity—is positive and large perform *worse* on tests than children of the same age assigned to classrooms where this age gap is smaller. Holding constant both own age and peer average age age, the authors do uncover some evidence that being relatively young by several different measures increases the likelihood of being retained in (forced to repeat a) grade, which is generally thought of as a signal of inadequate performance. One possible interpretation is that teachers assess a child's school readiness in relation to other children in a classroom, not by some absolute standard. However, their estimates suggest that moving a child from a classroom where he would be the oldest to one where he would be the youngest would still lower the likelihood of being retained on net.

CS surmise that their findings are driven by positive spillovers from having older classmates regardless of one's own age. For example, older classmates may be better behaved classmates, making time in the classroom more productive. If anything, these spillovers are likely to be especially large in this context because formal learning expectations of students were likely unchanging. Consistent with this idea, [researchers Todd] Elder and [Darren] Lubotsky show that, holding constant own age, having older peers in one's cohort because of a higher minimum age at school entry—which might also be associated with higher expectations of students—*increases* the likelihood of being retained or diagnosed with a learning disability, and while it raises test scores, does so by less than found by CS.

While CS make some headway toward estimating the contribution of relative age to the EAAG, they do not directly address the question of whether the EAAG might be driven by age at school entry or age at test. Elder and Lubotsky present suggestive evidence of the importance of age at test, showing that there is an "effect" of age at school entry on test scores at the start of the kindergarten year, before students have had much exposure to formal schooling. They also show that this age gradient is steeper for children from families with more resources, supporting the notion that age reflects the accumulation of investments in a child. To date, however, no research presents separate estimates of age at test and age at entry effects for the United States. However, [researchers Sandra] Black, [Paul] Devereux, and [Kjell] Salvanes take advantage of a situation in Norway, where time in school is roughly fixed, and age at school entry and age at test do not vary one-for-one. The authors find that age at test—not age at school entry—is largely responsible for the EAAG.

Implications of the Research

On balance, this new research suggests that the EAAG is largely an artifact of natural differences in skill between older and younger students. Does this mean that policy makers and parents should not be concerned about age at kindergarten entry? Not necessarily. There are possibly positive spillovers from having older peers, but these need to be weighed against the negative effects of starting school later. First, a lost year of schooling may lower test scores by more than is gained by an additional year of school preparation. Among minorities, high schoolers expected to be youngest in their school cohorts score significantly higher on tests than individuals expected to be eldest in the cohort behind them. Americans who are older when they start kindergarten also on average end up with less schooling as adults, since the oldest children in a class reach the age at which they can legally leave school in a lower grade. Further, under the assumption of an unchanging retirement age, the loss of labor market experience among older school entrants might not only negatively impact lifetime earnings, but also lower lifetime contributions to Social Security. Thus, knowing what drives the EAAG is only a first step toward learning the optimal age at kindergarten entry.

"Black artists like director Marion Mc-
Clinton and playwright Sam Roberson
... talk to [students] about theater as
a means to self-discovery and social
change but also remind them to do
their homework and stay on track for
college."

Arts Programs Help Narrow the Achievement Gap

Doug Belden

Doug Belden is the higher education reporter for the St. Paul communities served by the Pioneer Press *newspaper in Minnesota. The following viewpoint introduces readers to the students of the Seeds of Change program at Central High School, who were inspired to put on a play about the racial achievement gap at their school and ended up advancing their own academic careers in the process. The program recruits local theater professionals and college students to serve as artistic and academic mentors; participating in Seeds of Change has motivated students to stay focused on academic success and set higher goals for their accomplishments.*

As you read, consider the following questions:

1. According to the viewpoint author, how did the Seeds of Change theater project turn into a successful academic and social support system for participants?

2. As cited by the author, what specific improvements have Seeds of Change participants made in their own lives while working on the play?

3. What did the group leader James Williams learn about young people and success while working at a sporting goods store?

A black high school freshman hears his career plans ridiculed by his counselor. In the hallway, students taunt him with "You soft, n- - - -" and "All you gon' do is end up in jail." When he gets to class, the teacher is asking the students about their plans for the future. "To tell you the truth, I don't even know anymore," the boy says, and walks away.

The scene is part of an unusual theatrical project in development for more than a year at Central High School in St. Paul [Minnesota] and set to debut publicly next month [April 2008].

It started in the fall of 2006 with a challenge to the school's traveling theater troupe from district administrators to create a play illustrating St. Paul's racial achievement gap—the dramatic disparity in school performance between black students, especially males, and other student groups.

Reducing that gap is priority No. 1 in St. Paul and urban districts across the country, and the idea was to use the theater students' work to spark conversation around the issue in the district and the community.

The project soon passed to a smaller group of about 15—mostly black males—that became known as Seeds of Change.

As work on the play began, organizers realized they didn't want to put on a show about the achievement gap without first making sure the actors had their own academic houses in order.

So with help from $30,000 in grant money, college students were brought in this year for daily after-school tutoring and to help students talk to their teachers. Local theater artists were recruited as mentors. Half of each week's group meeting was devoted to checking in with the students and helping them with things like college applications and financial-aid forms.

As the actors prepare for their first performance April 16, the group has become at least as much academic and life-skills support group as artistic ensemble.

As group member Khymyle Mims put it: "We can't go put on a show and be what the show is."

It Is Never Too Late to Succeed

During check-in time at a Seeds of Change meeting last month, De'Andre Moss had some good news to share.

"I got a second job at Dairy Queen, he told the group of about a dozen students gathered in Central's basement theater for the weekly meeting. And on my last report card, I got all A's."

Hearing the grades, the group stood and clapped. What made the difference? asked teacher Jan Mandell.

"I just didn't stop. I just kept going," Moss said.

Moss had a 2.0 grade point average his first three years of high school, a C average. It didn't occur to him until recently that his grades might make it hard to get into college, he said, and he was afraid it was too late. That situation is typical for the young men in Seeds of Change.

"I actually thought I wasn't going to make it anywhere," Moss said. "I thought if I pushed myself, it would just be a waste of time."

But on his own initiative and with tutoring help in math from Concordia University student Michael Brooks, Moss brought his grades up.

"When I know what I'm doing in something, that motivates me to keep going," Moss said.

Moss said he was also fortunate that he got sick, oddly enough. He had to miss work, he said, which meant he finally had time to do his homework and visit with teachers after school for extra help.

Several Seeds students got "no credit" grades last semester, said Darlene Fry, a program manager for the district who helped set up Seeds of Change. Most improved in the second semester. None is currently failing, Fry said. Even better, "they're really talking about college in a more serious way," she said.

"It makes you push yourself to another level, because you have this group backing you up," said Mims. "We're not settling, basically."

At a meeting in late February, Mandell read off the names of about half a dozen Seeds students, including Mims, who made the B honor roll.

"The district wants proof? This is it," she said.

The Arts Provide a Platform—and an Audience—for Self-Expression

Much of the work of Seeds of Change has been identifying things like job schedules, family duties, transportation problems and the stigma of being labeled "smart" that get in the way of some black students succeeding in school.

But if the mood ever starts to veer into self-pity, James Williams is there to bring the students back sharply to their own responsibilities.

Williams, 53, a local actor and director known as "Jay Dub," serves as the group's primary mentor and creative resource.

The Why and How of Arts Integration Programs

Recent developments in cognitive science and neuroscience help explain the power of the arts. These developments have shown that . . . brain and body make up a single, fully integrated cognitive system. Scientists have found that most thought occurs on a level well below our conscious control and awareness and involves the processing of a continual stream of sensory information. We consistently represent the abstract through metaphors that we associate with physical experiences and emotions. . . .

What are their most salient principles and characteristics? The best programs

- Draw on the artistic resources of their communities, building sustained partnerships between schools and arts organizations and between teachers and artists.

- View student achievement and school improvement as pivotal to their mission—they are not only about advancing arts education.

- Engage artists, arts specialists, and teachers from all disciplines in serious inquiry about making powerful pedagogical and curricular links between the arts and other subjects.

- Use the arts as media to communicate content and as methods of learning. . . .

- Provide arts instruction both within the context of other subjects and as a subject in its own right.

Nick Rabkin and Robin Redmond,
"The Arts Make a Difference,"
Journal of Arts Management, Law, and Society, *Spring 2006.*

He is famous in Seeds for "the speech," part pep talk and part verbal butt-kicking delivered with a stern stare over the top of his glasses. Essentially, it's "about not wasting an opportunity," says Williams. "It comes down to: What are you willing to give up to accomplish your goal?"

A high school dropout who parlayed high test scores into a spot at Macalester College, Williams's world was opened up as a young man growing up in St. Louis when he got into theater.

The stage was the one place where he could speak his mind and have adults listen, he said.

"Someone would say, 'Oh wow, I've never seen it that way before,'" Williams said. "That's what I want these guys to find out."

Williams said he had an epiphany about the importance of guidance and mentorship when he was working at a sporting goods store.

He found himself spending a lot of time on the phone with 7-year-olds, going over the fine points of this piece of equipment or that. He wondered what was going on, and one day it dawned on him: The children's parents were with them on the end of the line, coaching them through the conversation as a way to prepare them for the sort of thing they would need to be able to handle in life.

"I started to realize how people were preparing their kids for success," he said.

One way or another, "young men are going to find a role model," Williams said.

In Seeds, they get to be in contact with him and other black artists like director Marion McClinton and playwright Sam Roberson, who talk to them about theater as a means to self-discovery and social change but also remind them to do their homework and stay on track for college.

"This thing that we've started can turn into 'There is no achievement gap,'" Williams told the students at the end of an especially productive rehearsal last month. "Ten years from now, they may be saying it's too many young black men from Central going to college.

"This is a big thing, y'all. This is a real big thing."

"You're creating your own legacy," said McClinton.

Can This Program Be Replicated?

With the amount of educational and artistic firepower being directed at a group that currently has about 20 students, it's not surprising Seeds of Change is showing results.

The question for the district is how the experience can be replicated.

On the one hand, Seeds is "totally organic to what's going on at that school," said Michael Thompson, the district's director of secondary curriculum. On the other, "we can learn a heckuva lot from what they've been doing," he said. "I think it would be great to have Seeds of Change planted all over the place."

Among the elements of Central's experiment that could be used elsewhere, Thompson said, are:

- Creation of a "safe space," where students can talk honestly and confidentially.

- Engagement with community members.

- Involvement of students with staff in helping teach other kids.

But whether or not the program eventually takes root in other schools, Seeds participants say they hope audiences this spring will come away with a better understanding of the pressures they face that contribute to the achievement gap, and perhaps a desire to help make things better.

The perceptions about young black men like the ones in Seeds are "totally opposite of who they are," said McClinton, whose son is a member of the group.

Spend time with them and "you learn them," he said. "Not 'young black males,' but this specific person, and you hear the same hopes and dreams that you've got."

He called Seeds "positive in just about every way you can think of. We have to dispel fear in this country."

The statistics on black student underperformance that group members were shown at the start of their process back in 2006 were shocking for some. But they weren't a surprise, said Karesa Pettis-Berry, one of the few young women in Seeds.

"People know that this is there," she said. "As a community, we all need to step up and say there's something going wrong. When you see a kid struggling, help."

Darrail Hughes said he hopes audiences take the play's message to heart.

"I want them to really look at what's causing these problems," he said. "Don't tune out, because this is really what's happening."

Adults always say they want to know what's going on with young people, Hughes said.

"Here's your chance. Listen up. We've done our part. Now you guys do yours."

Periodical Bibliography

The following articles have been selected to supplement the diverse views presented in this chapter.

Theresa Churchill and Valerie Wells | "Giving Students What They Need," *Herald-Review* (Decatur, IL), March 2, 2008.

Mary Ann Clark et al. | "Tackling Male Underachievement: Enhancing a Strengths-Based Learning Environment for Middle School Boys," *Professional School Counseling*, December 2008.

Patrick Coggins and Shawnrece Campbell | "Using Cultural Competence to Close the Achievement Gap," *Journal of Pan African Studies*, June 2008.

Kim Lamb Gregory | "Third Graders in Ventura Urged to Help One Another Learn," *Ventura County Star*, May 11, 2008.

Denise Johnson | "The Aggressive Educator," *Star-Tribune* (Minneapolis-St. Paul, MN), June 8, 2009.

Natasha Lindstrom | "Principal's Success at Poor School Captures National Attention," *Victorville Daily Press* (Victorville, CA), October 10, 2009.

Kim Marshall | "A How-To Plan for Widening the Gap: Decisions About Instruction Can Minimize or Maximize the Learning Gaps Between Groups of Students," *Phi Delta Kappan*, May 1, 2009.

William Roberts and Sergio Flores | "Strategies for Raising Achievement in Algebra," *Leadership*, January–February 2009.

Dorene D. Ross et al. | "Promoting Academic Engagement Through Insistence: Being a Warm Demander," *Childhood Education*, Spring 2008.

Hersh C. Waxman et al. | "Closing the Achievement Gap Within Reading and Mathematics Classrooms by Fostering Hispanic Students' Educational Resilience," *International Journal of Social Sciences*, Winter 2008.

CHAPTER 4

How Does Public Policy Affect the Achievement Gap?

Chapter Preface

On April 14, 1642, the Massachusetts Bay Colony was the first government in North America to enact compulsory education laws—all parents were responsible for ensuring that their children could read and write. The Puritan settlers who founded the colony believed that it was of supreme importance to their community's well-being that all its members be able to read the Bible and the civic laws that united them. As decades and then centuries passed, more colonies (and then states) adopted compulsory education policies, until 1918 when it was required in every state that all children complete elementary school.

Compulsory education was established in America for a variety of noneducational reasons. Perched at the start of the modern, global industrial era, the United States of the early twentieth century believed that universal literacy would strengthen America's international position of power. Compulsory education also accelerated the assimilation and acculturation of vast numbers of immigrant children into American culture, and curtailed the use of children as factory laborers, because they had to go to school instead.

Sweeping government policy has the great potential for change, and education law has been one of the most effective methods to transform society. Because the United States is more competitive on the international economic and political stage when its population is educated, it has always behooved the government to support equal access to education and to lessen the achievement gap between different groups of students. The 1944 Servicemen's Readjustment Act, also known as the GI Bill, paid for returning war veterans to pursue job training and higher education and to receive loans to buy houses, which helped offset the economic disaster of returning servicemen competing for the same jobs and leveraged thousands of people from the working into the professional class with college degrees and home ownership. In 1954, the Supreme Court case *Brown v. Board of Education of Topeka* paved the way for radical improvements in the education of black students, and members of other minority groups, and made the available pool of laborers and innovators much larger. In 1972, Title IX of the Education Amendments practically doubled it again by opening up the math and sciences to girls who were interested.

Federal spending has expanded school infrastructure, too, allowing educators and administrators to better serve their students by simply offering more resources. In 1946, President Truman signed into law the National School Lunch Act to provide free or subsidized lunches to needy children, which improved student performance partly by increasing attendance and partly because hungry children cannot concentrate very well on their lessons. The Cold War-era Space Race between the United States and the Soviet Union prompted a surge of federal money for science and mathematics training, so that Americans would not fall behind the technological skills of their ideological enemies and possibly fall prey to aggressive, better-equipped red armies; schools that would not have been able to afford laboratories and materials could now provide enhanced math and science curricula. Currently, student loans and educational grants enable hundreds of thousands of college students to pay for tuition, books, and housing at public and private universities each year.

The following chapter describes some of the other public policies in place to reduce or eliminate the achievement gap and improve American life by making education more equitable and more accessible to groups of students from every race and socioeconomic status.

> *"Gains in test scores have far outweighed declines since NCLB [No Child Left Behind] took effect."*

The No Child Left Behind Act Has Increased Student Achievement

Naomi Chudowsky, Victor Chudowsky, and Nancy Kober

Naomi Chudowsky researches educational testing and has worked for the state of Connecticut and the U.S. Department of Education on the development of student assessments. Victor Chudowsky is a public policy research consultant; Nancy Kober researches, writes, and edits for the Center on Education Policy (CEP). The following viewpoint is excerpted from their report Answering the Question that Matters Most: Has Student Achievement Increased Since No Child Left Behind? *The authors explain that test score data from all fifty states reveal that most have experienced improvement in student performance since the No Child Left Behind Act was passed by Congress in 2002.*

Naomi Chudowsky, Victor Chudowsky, and Nancy Kober, *Answering the Question that Matters Most: Has Student Achievement Increased Since No Child Left Behind?* Washington, DC: Center on Education Policy, 2007. Reproduced by permission.

As you read, consider the following questions:

1. What academic subject did most states show most improvement in since the No Child Left Behind Act was instituted, as cited by the authors?

2. As presented by the authors, what trends in the improvement of reading at the high school level are evident in the collected data?

3. How might the practice of "teaching to the test" influence the positive results in assessment of student progress since 2002, according to the authors?

The weight of evidence indicates that state test scores in reading and mathematics have increased overall since NCLB [No Child Left Behind] was enacted. All of our analyses—including percentages of students scoring proficient, effect sizes (a measure based on average, or mean, test scores), and pre- and post-NCLB trends—found substantially more states with gains in student test results than with declines since 2002.

Regardless of whether one analyzes percentages proficient or effect sizes, the number of states showing achievement gains since 2002 is far greater than the number showing declines. (The subset of states with sufficient data varies, depending on the particular analysis.) For example, of the 24 states with both percentage proficient and effect size data for middle school reading, 11 states demonstrated moderate-to-large gains in this subject and grade span, while only one state exhibited a moderate or larger decline. Using percentage proficient data alone, 20 of the 39 states with this type of data showed moderate-to-large gains in middle school reading, while only one state showed a moderate or larger decline.

Of the 22 states with both percentage proficient and effect size data, five made moderate-to-large gains in reading and math across all grade spans (elementary, middle, and high school) according to both measures. In other words, these five states showed gains according to all of the indicators collected for this study, allowing one to conclude with some confidence that achievement has gone up in those states. In reading, seven states showed moderate-to-large increases across all grades analyzed, according to both the percentage proficient and effect size measures. In math, nine states showed similar gains across all grades analyzed on both measures. (The group of seven and the group of eight states include the five states that made gains in both subjects.) The rest of the states had different trends at different grade spans.

Elementary-level math is the area in which the most states showed improvements. Of the 25 states with both percentage proficient and effect size data in elementary math, 22 demonstrated moderate-to-large math gains at the elementary level on both measures, while none showed moderate or larger declines. Based on percentages proficient alone, 37 of the 41 states with trend data in elementary math demonstrated moderate-to-large math gains, while none showed declines of that magnitude.

More states showed declines in reading and math achievement at the high school level than at the elementary or middle school levels. Still, the number of states with test score gains in high school exceeded the number with declines.

Since many states had reform efforts well under way before NCLB, it is useful to know whether the pace of improvement has picked up or slowed down since NCLB took effect in 2002. Only 13 states supplied enough years of data for us to make this determination. In nine of these states, test results improved at a greater yearly rate after 2002 than before. In the other four states, the pre-NCLB rate of average yearly gain outstripped the post-NCLB rate. . . .

Average Yearly Gains in Academic Progress

How much progress have states made in raising their percentages proficient? Since a certain amount of year-to-year fluctuation in test scores is normal, it is often more meaningful to look at average yearly gains than to simply compare one year's percentage proficient with another's. (The average yearly gain or decline is determined by computing the cumulative change over a period of years and dividing by the number of years.)

For each of the grade spans with two or more years of comparable data (the minimum period needed to compute average yearly gains), we calculated the median of states' average yearly gains since 2002. (The median is a sort of midpoint; an equal number of states fall above or below the median.) In reading, the median of states' average yearly gains in percentage proficient since 2002 was 1.8 percentage points per year at the elementary level, and 1.0 percentage points at both the middle and high school levels. In math, the median of states' average yearly gains was notably higher—3.0 percentage points per year at the elementary level, 2.1 at the middle school level, and 1.8 at the high school level. Above and below the median, the average yearly gains in individual states covered a wide spectrum. In elementary reading, the average yearly gains in percentages proficient ranged from a minimum of –2.2 percentage points (in other words, a decline) in one state to a maximum of +10.0 percentage points in another. In high school reading the range of average yearly gains was even broader—from a minimum of –2.9 percentage points (a decline) in one state to a maximum +18.0 percentage points in another.

Test Score Trends in Reading and Math Since 2002

In addition to analyzing broad trends across grades and subjects, we also took a closer look at separate achievement trends in reading and in math since 2002.

Reading Trends

In reading, performance has increased since 2002. As already noted, seven states showed gains in reading across all

Donations Help Make NCLB Gains Possible

Hamilton County (Tennessee) has relied on foundations to help finance extra work at many of its schools. A $5 million grant from the Benwood Foundation paid for extra professional development at nine of the system's lowest-performing schools, which are poor, urban and mostly minority. The foundation extended its support by $725,000 to continue the initiative through this school year. The Osborne Foundation donated $1.5 million to enable 100 teachers at the Benwood schools to earn free master's degrees at the University of Tennessee at Chattanooga. The Urban League and Community Impact Fund paid for specialists to work in the schools, engaging parents in their children's educations. And Community Education Alliance, created by former Chattanooga mayor and U.S. Sen.-elect Bob Corker, paid for bonuses for teachers and principals who raised student achievement by a certain amount each year. The investment has produced exceptional results, said Dan Challener, president of the Public Education Foundation, which administered the grants. "The Benwood schools outgained 90 percent of schools in Tennessee and made a significant step toward closing the achievement gap in Hamilton County," he said.

Christina Cooke, "The Gap Narrows:
Test Scores Advanced for Disadvantaged Students,"
Chattanooga Times Free Press, *December 3, 2006.*

three grade spans in both percentages proficient and effect sizes. Based on percentages proficient alone, nine states demonstrated moderate-to-large increases across the three grade spans.

Within the same grade span, more states demonstrated increases in reading than declines. For example, based on both percentage proficient and effect size data, 14 states showed moderate-to-large gains at the elementary level, while just one state showed a decline. Based on percentages proficient alone, 29 states experienced moderate-to-large gains in elementary reading, while only two states experienced moderate-to-large declines.

Fewer states made improvements in reading at the high school level than at other grade levels. Based on both percentage proficient and effect size data, two states showed moderate-to-large declines at high school. Based solely on percentages proficient, four states experienced high school declines.

Mathematics Trends

In math, performance has also increased since 2002. Nineteen states showed moderate-to-large gains in percentages proficient across all grade spans in math; among them were the nine states with gains across all grade spans in effect sizes, as well.

Within the same grade span, more states experienced gains in math than declines. Of the states with both percentage proficient and effect size data, 22 showed moderate-to-large gains in math at the elementary school level, while none had declines. As with reading, improvements at the high school level were less striking than at other grade spans; only 12 states showed moderate-to-large gains at the high school level.

Results in math were most impressive at the elementary level. Based on proficiency data alone, 37 of the 41 states with sufficient data showed at least moderate gains in elementary math.

Possible Explanations for Trends Since 2002

Our evidence shows that gains in state test scores have far outweighed declines since NCLB took effect. Below we offer some possible explanations for the increases. The list is not exhaustive, but these are the explanations most often mentioned in research on test trends. Any or all of these factors in combination may be contributing to these trends. Moreover, different explanations could apply to different states or school districts within states.

- *Increased learning.* One likely reason for the upward trends in state test scores is that students are learning more and consequently are doing better on state tests. Administrators and teachers have made major efforts to improve achievement, according to CEP's [Center on Education Policy's] case studies and nationally representative survey of school districts. According to this year's district survey, the following four strategies were most often considered successful in raising achievement in Title I schools identified for improvement under NCLB: hiring additional teachers to reduce class size (cited as at least somewhat successful by 97% of districts with such schools), providing assistance through school support teams (95%), increasing the quality and quantity of teacher and principal professional development (92%), and aligning curriculum and instruction with standards and/or assessments (91%), however, it is not possible to sort out how much of the impetus for these types of changes has come from NCLB and how much from state and local reforms. In CEP's surveys, roughly seven of ten district respondents cited school district programs and policies unrelated to NCLB as important causes of improved achievement in reading and math, and more than a third cited state programs and policies.

- *Teaching to the test.* Teaching to the test can be a positive practice when it means aligning curricula to well-designed standards and tests and ensuring that classroom teaching covers the most important knowledge and skills contained in those standards. Teaching to the test can have adverse effects, however, if it means narrowing the curriculum to include only the subjects, topics, and skills that are likely to appear on state tests. This latter practice can raise test scores without also improving students' mastery of the broader subject being tested. It can give the false impression that student achievement is rising when students are actually learning the same amount or less; this is sometimes referred to as "score inflation." CEP's past district surveys and case studies found evidence that many school districts are reducing time in other subjects to allow more time for reading and math.

- *More lenient tests, scoring, or data analyses.* We were careful not to compare test data when we were aware of breaks in comparability due to major changes in testing systems. But . . . test results can still be subtly manipulated through a series of small decisions that affect such factors as equating, scoring, and proficiency levels and that amount to tinkering rather than substantial alterations. Faced with intense pressure to show achievement gains, state education officials may be likely to err on the side of leniency when making these types of decisions. It is difficult to find evidence of these types of subtle changes to state testing programs; however, we do know that some of the changes that states have made to their NCLB accountability plans have increased the numbers of students counted as proficient.

- *Changes in populations tested.* Changes in the student population tested from year to year can affect aggregate state test scores. To cite one example, if significantly more students are held back in grade, it could appear that achievement in a particular grade has increased from one year to the next; for instance, the students who are retained in 4th grade may do better on the 4th-grade tests after repeating a grade, while the cohort of students in 5th grade will not include the lowest-achieving students who had not been promoted. To cite a contrasting example, if one year's cohort of test-takers includes a significantly higher proportion from histori-cally low-performing subgroups, such as limited-English-proficient students, than the previous year's cohort did, achievement may appear to decrease in the aggregate, but the apparent decrease is a consequence of demography rather than learning. . . .

Main Findings About Pre- and Post-NCLB Comparisons

Nine of the 13 states with pre- and post-NCLB achievement data made greater average yearly gains after NCLB took effect than before, by most indicators. The other four states showed slower progress after NCLB took effect, by most indicators. It is difficult to say, however, whether the small sample of 13 states represents a true national trend of hastening progress after NCLB. For now, these comparisons should be taken as suggestive.

In most states with complete data, the effect size and per-centage proficient comparisons of pre- and post-NCLB trends were consistent. In a few instances, however, effect size data contradicted the percentage proficient data. In Kentucky for grade 11 math and in Louisiana for grades four and eight reading, the percentage proficient results showed greater aver-age yearly gains after NCLB than before, but effect size results at those grades showed greater gains before NCLB than after. In New Jersey, gains in percentages proficient for grade eight reading were higher after NCLB than before, but effect sizes showed average yearly declines that were larger after NCLB than before. Clearly, one would have more confidence in con-cluding that gains have been greater after NCLB in a state like

Kansas, where 12 of 12 indicators show the same general trend, than in a state like Louisiana, which showed a mixed pattern.

Possible Explanations for Pre- and Post-NCLB Trends

Possible explanations for higher post-NCLB gains in the nine states are the same as those given in the achievement trends above—greater student learning, more intensive teaching to the test, and changes in test administration, or a combination of these factors.

Changes in the population of students tested may be a particularly important factor for comparisons between pre- and post-NCLB trends. The trends could be skewed in favor of pre-NCLB results because of changes in the number of students included in testing. NCLB requires that 95% of students be tested, including students with disabilities and limited-English-proficient students. Before NCLB, fewer than 95% of students might have been tested. In particular, these two subgroups with special needs may have been left out of testing more often, along with students with attendance problems. This may help explain why four states showed greater gains before NCLB.

> "NCLB [No Child Left Behind] is lead-
> ing to further segregation as inner-city
> schools find themselves faced with pu-
> nitive remedies that do not actually im-
> prove the schools, increase student
> learning, or raise test scores."

The No Child Left Behind Act Has Widened the Achievement Gap

Liz Hollingworth

Liz Hollingworth is an assistant professor at the University of Iowa College of Education and the Department of Educational Policy and Leadership Studies. The following viewpoint describes the No Child Left Behind (NCLB) education reform act. Hollingworth argues that NCLB's systems of high-stakes testing and school sanctions/rewards increase the achievement gap between white and black Americans. She places the problem against the backdrop of historical racism and discrimination and points out that although NCLB purports to be color blind, the problems faced by black students in a culture that denies racism leave them outside NCLB's sphere of positive influence.

Liz Hollingworth, "Unintended Educational and Social Consequences of the No Child Left Behind Act," *The Journal of Gender, Race, & Justice*, April 4, 2008, pp. 311–326. Reproduced by permission.

As you read, consider the following questions:

1. According to Eduardo Bonilla-Silva, on what basis do white Americans explain the failure of black Americans (and members of other minority groups) to succeed?

2. As cited by the author, how have many schools adapted their instructional curriculum to address the requirements of NCLB test scores?

3. How has NCLB affected the ability of special education teachers to work with struggling students, as explained by the author?

The rules and regulations of the No Child Left Behind Act (NCLB or "the Act") have not reduced the gap in student academic achievement as much as Congress originally intended. The great promise of NCLB is that, once held accountable, schools will finally focus on the education of low-achieving students, thus reducing the gap in student academic achievement between white students and African American, Hispanic, and Native American student populations. Congress devised a series of punishments and rewards designed to encourage schools to find innovative ways to reach the children that schools have historically "left behind" in traditional public education. The creators of NCLB intended the Act to provide schools with rewards and punishments, in an effort to encourage schools to give extra assistance to the poor and minority students that public schools traditionally allowed to struggle or drop out. The punishments provided in the Act range from the loss of federal Title I funding to complete school takeovers. The rewards include additional money for after-school programs and increased teacher pay for performance.

However, the way in which the Act has been implemented has failed to promote the Act's initial goals. Despite the ideology that schools should be held accountable for unequal academic progress, children who attend inner-city schools with the highest poverty rates must still overcome the second-rate education they receive in overcrowded classrooms in school facilities that are badly in need of repair. This disconnect between the goals of the Act and the real-world consequences of its implementation may be due to the current policy focus on student testing as the primary remedy for the achievement gap. . . .

Color Blindness, Race, and NCLB

One of the stated goals of NCLB is to close the achievement gap between white and minority children. In pursuit of this goal, NCLB counterintuitively applies a "color-blind" approach to education reform. Color-blind public policies claim to treat individuals of all races equally based on a system of merit. However, recent scholarship asserts that these policies simply replace pigment-based racism with culturally based racism. As a result, the implementation of policies based on this color-blind approach perpetuate the existing inequality between the white majority and minorities in the United States. Consequently, NCLB's provisions consistent with a policy of color blindness virtually ensure that the Act will fail in its goal to close the existing achievement gap between white and minority students.

Michael Omi and Howard Winant provide a description of the roots of public support for NCLB's color-blind reform policy in their historical text, *Racial Formation in the United States: from the 1960s to the 1990s*. Omi and Winant theorize that race is an ideological construct, and they trace the way that race functions in America from the civil rights movement in the 1960s to the 1980s and 1990s, when the predominant view of racial equality shifted politically. Voices from the conservative Right claimed that affirmative action and social programs that legitimated group rights were actually shifting racial discrimination to white males. The newly fashioned transformation under the [Bill] Clinton administration was a vision of a "'color-blind' society where racial considerations were never entertained in the selection of leaders, in hiring decisions, and in the distribution of goods and services in general." Under the neoconservative [George W.] Bush administration, racial ideology has been transformed into a set of public policies that is essentially blind to race, particularly with respect to postsecondary education and race preference for admission.

This vision of color blindness as a means of eliminating racial discrimination is founded on the seemingly paradoxical notion that it is noble to ignore race while simultaneously honoring diversity. As Omi and Winant observed, the appeal of this ideology is not simply about "fairness," but also about the maintenance of existing social positions and political stability. Similarly, Eduardo Bonilla-Silva writes about color-blind racism, white racial ideology in the United States, and the postmodern support of the racial status quo. The dominant frames of color-blind racial matters are subtle, and many whites do not believe that racism is a problem in today's United States. He writes that "because whites believe that discrimination is no longer a salient factor in the United States, they believe that blacks' plight is the result of blacks' cultural deficiencies (e.g., laziness, lack the proper values, and disorganized family life.)" In other words, it is the opinion, of many whites that different immigrant groups in American history have managed their success not because of the whiteness of their skin, but because of their ability to pull themselves up by their figurative bootstraps more effectively than immigrants with darker skin. . . .

Unintended Consequences of Accountability

The single-minded concentration on school improvement policies that use punishments and rewards based on student test scores has had unintended educational and social consequences. Not only have teachers and school administrators shifted the curricular focus in an effort to raise test scores, but in some cases they have also abandoned thoughtful, research-based classroom practices in exchange for test preparation. The unintended consequences of these reforms have acted to subvert the primary goals of NCLB.

Shifts in the Enacted Curriculum in the Classroom

What is new about the present version of the ESEA [Elementary and Secondary Education Act] is the focus on accountability. Schools are now subjected to a loss of funding (i.e., Title I) if the reading, math, and science test scores of traditionally low-achieving students are not raised to the proficient level. As a result, schools that are struggling to raise test scores are narrowing the curriculum and abandoning innovative interdisciplinary curricula to focus on math, reading, and science because of high-stakes testing. Other important curricular areas (e.g., history, music, physical education, and art) are not part of the accountability system for schools and are therefore receiving short shrift. The Center on Education Policy surveyed 299 school districts and reported that seventy-one percent of schools had reduced instructional time in one or more subjects to increase the time spent on reading and math because of the pressures of NCLB. In Jonathan Kozol's book, *The Shame of the Nation*, he writes that "in some schools, the principals and teachers tell me that the tests themselves and preparation for the tests control more than a quarter of the year."

Increased Segregation

As educators like Kozol have noted, NCLB is leading to further segregation as inner-city schools find themselves faced with punitive remedies that do not actually improve the schools, increase student learning, or raise test scores. The options that have not worked include: restructuring the school administration, replacing teaching staff, providing school choice for families, and requiring mandatory tutoring programs. The end result is that schools serving students from low socioeconomic areas in this country are faced with fewer financial resources for more limited academic programs, which is precisely the opposite effect the ESEA was intended to have on public education for low-income children.

Wasting Existing, Thoughtful Programs

Worse still, states like Iowa that already had thoughtful, voluntary diagnostic assessment systems in place have had to abandon them to be in compliance with NCLB. Linda Darling-Hammond, a Stanford professor and outspoken critic of the NCLB legislation, writes that a number of states have replaced "instructionally rich, improvement-oriented systems with more rote-oriented punishment-driven approaches—and it has thrown many high-performing and steadily improving schools into chaos rather than helping them remain focused and deliberate in their ongoing efforts to serve students well." This is a tragic and ironic consequence of the legislation— that teachers and schools would be undermined in the school improvement work to which school improvement legislation committed them.

Unintended Effects on Teachers

No Child Left Behind has also caused unintended effects on the teaching workforce, particularly in schools with the Schools in Need of Assistance (SINA) designation. Highly qualified teachers with experience are leaving high-poverty schools, especially when teacher salaries are tied to student academic performance, which reinforces the unequal educational opportunities. "Nearly 40% of all teachers leaving high-poverty schools reported either job dissatisfaction or the de-

Capitalist Greed Is Destroying Public Education: A Manifesto

Unchecked capitalism is destroying our nation's public schools, and No Child Left Behind (NCLB) is the final nail in their coffin. Marching under the banner of "accountability," right-wing, pro-business forces are willfully undermining the democratic right of all children to a free, high-quality education. . . .

No system of schools—public or private—has ever demonstrated that it can close this poverty-induced learning gap for most children. If policy makers know this—and they surely must—they ignore it. In fact, in the two decades preceding No Child Left Behind, a succession of presidents and congresses gradually abandoned historically successful Great Society programs that had lifted many of the poor out of poverty. Today, more than one-quarter of American children live in poverty, more than in any other industrialized nation.

At the same time, those in the corporate elite and their political allies have ratcheted up the pressure on schools with a harsh accountability system that they have consistently shunned for themselves. Can you imagine applying to Enron and the Wall Street financial manipulators who brought us the credit and home foreclosure crises the same punitive standards we now apply to the schools? . . .

Richard Gibboney, "Why an Undemocratic
Capitalism Has Brought Public Education to Its Knees,"
Phi Delta Kappan, *September 2008.*

sire to pursue a better job or improve job opportunities as a reason for departing." The definition of a Highly Qualified Teacher (HQT) according to NCLB is someone who:

Has full state certification as a teacher and does not have certification or licensure requirements waived on an emergency, temporary, or provisional basis; holds a minimum of a bachelor's degree; and has demonstrated subject matter competency in each of the academic subjects in which the teacher teaches, in a manner in compliance with Section 9101(23) of ESEA and determined by the state.

Further regulations associated with the HQT have clarified that a teacher must hold a bachelor's degree in the subject that they are assigned to teach. An unforeseen result of this definition has been that Special Education teachers, who have special credentials and training in how to teach special needs students, do not generally hold bachelor's degrees in every subject they teach. As a result, they are labeled "unqualified" to teach anything outside of the subject in which they hold their degree.

Many teachers, demoralized from the HQT provisions, would also argue that the law employs a view of motivation that they find objectionable. Nel Noddings argues that "as educators, we would not use threats, punishments, and pernicious comparisons to 'motivate' our students, but that is how the No Child Left Behind law treats the school establishment." Noddings opines that "a good law does not demoralize good people."

Diversion of Resources to Testing Instead of Teaching

Perhaps the most shocking effect of NCLB has been the diversion of resources (i.e., education dollars) to testing. This has led to capacity building, in which new state bureaucracies manage large-scale testing programs and report to the federal Department of Education. The United States General Accounting Office [now the Government Accountability Office] reported that between $1.9 billion and $5.3 billion (depending on the item type selected) would be spent on state testing programs between 2002–08. As educational policy analysts have observed, the spending on assessment has often been at the expense of building repairs and facility maintenance. Indeed, NCLB prescribes the budget expenditures from the federal funds, and as a result, as Darling-Hammond notes, "most of the federal money has to be spent for purposes other than upgraded facilities, textbooks, or teachers' salaries."

Conclusions

NCLB's focus on gaps between different groups of students is both novel and important. However, the policy of academic achievement testing as a remedy for the social and economic problems that have plagued our schools has not evened the playing field for our children in failing schools. As Congress debates the best strategies for reforming NCLB in this election year, we need to be wary of policy innovations that amount to simply rearranging the deck chairs on the *Titanic*. We need to be prepared to rethink the paradigm that tells policy makers that high-stakes testing is an adequate tool for school reform. What is more, we need to be ready to have the hard conversations about race and ideology in this country before we are going to truly be prepared to close the achievement gaps. This cannot happen when we ignore white privilege and lump together the problems of the poor children with the problems of minority children, as if these two are always intertwined.

The persistence of the achievement gap between white and minority children in our public schools has more to do with the inequities in social opportunities than it does with the need for more educational testing. But it is much easier to insist that teachers and students need more carrots and sticks to keep them from being so lazy than it is to say that major social reform cannot occur until we confront the issues of race and class head-on, and not merely expect schools to be the institution that can cure the social problems that face our youngest generation. Social remedies like NCLB that fail to recognize this are doomed to fail.

> "Many sophisticated statistical analyses
> of U.S. voucher programs have found
> that enrollment in private voucher
> schools has led to student achievement
> gains in one or more subject areas."

School Vouchers Narrow the Achievement Gap

Andrew Coulson

Andrew Coulson is the director of the Cato Institute's Center for Educational Freedom, an organization founded on the principle that parents—not the government or educators—are the people best suited to make decisions about the education of children. The following viewpoint first appeared as a chapter in the book What America Can Learn from School Choice in Other Countries, *a look at how free market choice of schools can improve standards of education. Coulson presents examples of voucher programs in Chile and the Netherlands that decrease the achievement gap among students of different class backgrounds.*

As you read, consider the following questions:

1. What critique does the viewpoint author make of the Hsieh and Urquiola research that found a widening of the achievement gap after school vouchers were implemented in Chile?

2. According to the author, what are the likely immediate effects of the implementation of a private school voucher system?

3. What did researcher Jesse Levin discover about students of lower socioeconomic status attending private Dutch Catholic schools?

On its Web site, the National Education Association (NEA) makes the unequivocal assertion that "there is no evidence that vouchers improve student learning. Every serious study of voucher plans has concluded that vouchers do not improve student achievement."

Although there is certainly ongoing controversy over the significance and validity of the U.S. school voucher research, the NEA's assertion is patently mistaken. Many sophisticated statistical analyses of U.S. voucher programs have found that enrollment in private voucher schools has led to student achievement gains in one or more subject areas. Nevertheless, the NEA's view on this subject is widely shared. An online article by the managing editor of the public school advocacy publication *Rethinking Schools* is titled "Vouchers and the False Promise of Academic Achievement." In this piece, editor Barbara Miner writes:

> Conservatives have spinned [*sic*] vouchers as a way to increase achievement for low-income minorities. And clearly, reducing the black/white academic achievement gap is one of this country's highest educational priorities. But the academic case for vouchers rests on rhetoric, not reality.

The Applied Research Center goes one step further, asserting that "a voucher system in California would only exacerbate educational inequity. The primary beneficiaries of vouchers are people who already have resources." That is also the view of Stanford University professor Bruce Fuller, whose "results suggest that school choice may inadvertently exacerbate stratification and inequality."

One of the most thoroughly researched and argued presentations of this criticism is a paper by World Bank researchers Chang-Tai Hsieh and Miguel Urquiola. Hsieh and Urquiola examined data from the first eight years of the Chilean voucher program and concluded that it succeeded only in redistributing wealthier and higher-achieving students to the private sector and not in improving overall student performance.

In weighing those criticisms, context ... is key. We must keep in mind that wealth and academic achievement are already correlated under the current U.S. public school system. In fact, among the education systems of all 27 nations belonging to the Organisation for Economic Co-operation and Development (OECD), U.S. public schools show the single strongest correlation between wealth and achievement.

So how would the introduction of a universal school choice program likely affect overall student achievement and the distribution of student achievement? An obvious jumping-off point for answering those questions is to review the conclusions of Hsieh and Urquiola. They rest their case, essentially, on five findings:

- In 1988 achievement was higher in well-established private schools than in newly created private schools (implying, the authors believe, that established schools had already snapped up the wealthier and hence higher-achieving students, leaving newer schools with the remaining poorer, lower-achieving students).

- After controlling for observable school and community characteristics, districts with a higher private enrollment share do not differ significantly from other districts in math scores, repetition rates, or student attainment (i.e., years of school completed).

- After controls, districts with higher growth in private enrollment share between 1982 and 1988 do not differ significantly in educational outcomes from districts in which private enrollment grew more modestly.

- Nationwide, "average test scores did not change," though repetition rates did fall somewhat and school attainment did rise somewhat.

- Chile dropped one place in the international ranking of countries participating in the 1970 and 1999 international tests of mathematics and science.

Addressing Concerns About Vouchers in Chile

Contrary to the researchers' assertions, it does not necessarily follow from those findings that private voucher schools are no more effective than public schools or that the school voucher program has failed to improve overall student achievement. By looking only at the first six years of the program, the authors neglect to consider several important realities. Newly created organizations tend to have more problems than well-established ones. It is possible that, as poorly managed start-ups either went out of business or eventually improved their operations, overall private school achievement may have gone up. It is also conceivable that public schools may have been slow to react to declining enrollment in an academically effective way. Second, the introduction of a voucher program was not the only major change in government education policy during the 1980s. Total government spending also fell substantially in real terms during that decade, and that could have had a deleterious effect on achievement. Government spending began to recover only in the 1990s. Finally, it is not clear whether the cited decline in the relative international performance of Chilean students occurred between 1970 and 1982 (before the voucher program was introduced) or between 1982 and 1999 (after it was introduced).

One way to address the above concerns is to look at the performance of Chilean schools from 1988 onward. Unfortunately, it is impossible to discern reliable year-to-year test score trends before 1997 because results of the national SIMCE [Chilean system for measuring educational quality] test were not guaranteed to be comparable from year to year prior to that date. Despite that limitation, Francisco Gallego of the Chilean Central Bank has come up with an excellent alternative statistic. Instead of charting the annual test score changes of voucher schools or public schools, Gallego decided to compare how well each type of school has performed compared with elite non-voucher private schools—expensive private schools that have not participated in the nation's voucher program (because their tuitions exceed the voucher amount).

Gallego found that both private voucher schools and public schools steadily improved in comparison with the elite non-voucher private schools from 1988 all the way through the most recent (year 2000) data. In 1988, fourth-grade students in public schools scored only 64.7 percent as well as students in elite non-voucher schools, but by 2000 they were scoring 81.1 percent as well as elite non-voucher students. Private voucher schools also improved substantially relative to elite non-voucher schools, rising from 74.0 percent to 87.4 percent of the elite non-voucher schools' performance.

Transitioning to a Voucher System

Another pattern that emerges when we look beyond the voucher program's early tumultuous years is that schools created in response to the program eventually closed the achievement gap with schools that predated it. In the words of researchers Claudio Sapelli and Bernardita Vial:

> Pre-reform schools are significantly better than post-reform schools in 1989, but the difference halves in 1993 and disappears in 1997. In 1997 both pre- and post-reform [private] schools are significantly better than municipal [i.e., public] schools.

Several studies have shown that Chile's private voucher schools outperform public schools, after controlling for student and family background. Some, but not all, of those studies have found that the private-sector advantage is concentrated among Catholic schools and that secular private schools perform at roughly the same level as public schools. No studies have found that public schools outperform private voucher schools overall. As noted earlier, Sapelli and Vial revealed that most public schools receive substantial government funding over and above the voucher, which private schools do not receive. Their study concluded that public schools that spend only modestly more than the value of the voucher perform significantly worse than both private voucher schools and high-spending public schools.

The Chilean experience thus suggests that there may be an initial period following the introduction of a universal choice program during which performance may not improve because of the preponderance of new and untested schools and the shock to public schools of rapidly falling enrollments. After this period the system seems to stabilize and performance improves, especially in the private sector.

If this experience is generally representative of large-scale choice programs, then the long-established voucher program in the Netherlands should be showing strong academic achievement, and if its private schools perform better than its public schools, that should be because of their superior quality and not simply the result of a more select student body.

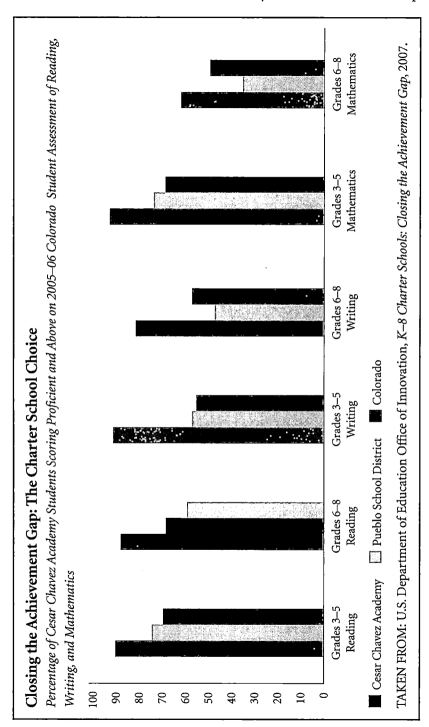

Closing the Achievement Gap: The Charter School Choice

Percentage of Cesar Chavez Academy Students Scoring Proficient and Above on 2005–06 Colorado Student Assessment of Reading, Writing, and Mathematics

TAKEN FROM: U.S. Department of Education Office of Innovation, *K–8 Charter Schools: Closing the Achievement Gap*, 2007.

Dutch Voucher Programs Close the Gap

Of the 20 nations participating in the Third International Mathematics and Science Study (TIMSS), the Netherlands consistently scored in the top three in both subjects, at both the eighth- and the twelfth-grade levels. When fourth graders in 35 countries were tested for reading ability in 2001, students in the Netherlands placed second, behind students in Sweden (another country with a school choice program, albeit a more limited one). Young adults in the Netherlands also scored well in literacy on the International Adult Literacy Survey of the mid-1990s, once again coming in second behind Sweden.

From the standpoint of overall achievement, therefore, the Dutch experience is consistent with the emergent trend in Chile. But what about the relative performance of private voucher schools and public schools in the Netherlands? For historical reasons explained above, the vast majority of private schools in Holland are either Catholic or Protestant. A 2002 study by Jesse Levin reports that raw test scores for private Protestant schools are slightly, but not statistically significantly, better overall than raw test scores for public schools. Private Catholic schools, by contrast, show significantly better raw scores in most of the grades and subjects tested. To determine if this achievement difference was genuine or simply an artifact of a more elite clientele, Levin controlled for a variety of student and family background characteristics. He found that Dutch Catholic schools enroll students of *lower* overall socioeconomic status, not higher status as the cream-skimming argument would suppose. As a result, the raw score advantage of Catholic schools over public schools in Holland actually *understates* the benefit of attending a private Catholic school.

According to a research survey by Jaap Dronkers, private religious schools across Europe, most of which receive some government funding, generally perform better than public schools. He writes:

The importance of the effectiveness differences in the cognitive domains indicates that educational systems with public and state-funded religious schools give parents a real choice between schools of different quality. Given the higher general level of achievements in both public and religious schools of European societies and the smaller differences between [the] achievement of these schools within European societies compared to the average achievement of public schools and the between-school differences in the USA, it is difficult to argue that the parental choice in these European societies has increased inequality within these societies or lowered the level of schooling.

This pattern of private-sector academic superiority is not limited to religious schools or to wealthy Europe. The overwhelming majority of studies find that private schools operating in competitive markets across the developing world are more academically effective, more efficient, and more responsive to the curricular demands of parents than are state-run public schools. In a recent review of this research, I discovered 16 studies indicating superior private school academic achievement, 3 findings indicating no significant difference between the sectors, and only 1 finding showing a public school advantage. . . .

The Evidence Supports Vouchers

The belief that universal education markets would fail to improve overall academic achievement and exacerbate the achievement gap between the haves and have-nots is not borne out by the evidence. After its first tumultuous years, the Chilean voucher program allowed students in both public schools and private voucher schools to substantially narrow the gap with their wealthier peers in non-voucher private schools. Though before and after trend data are not available for the long-established Dutch voucher system, the Netherlands' consistent ranking among the top-achieving nations at least suggests that competition and parental choice are consistent with strong academic success. Furthermore, the fact that Dutch Catholic schools score higher than Dutch public schools, despite enrolling students of *lower* socioeconomic status, suggests that the critics have things exactly backward.

This study, by itself, is of course not definitive. There was not space to examine every relevant case, and there are other criticisms of market education not treated here. Nevertheless, it is hoped that the evidence discussed here will facilitate sound, empirically based education decision making by U.S. policy makers.

"The analysis revealed . . . no significant achievement impacts in reading or math for students who came from SINI [schools identified as in need of improvement] schools."

School Vouchers Do Not Narrow the Achievement Gap

Patrick Wolf et al.

Patrick Wolf is the 21st Century Chair in School Choice in the Department of Education Reform at the University of Arkansas' College of Education and Health Professions. The following viewpoint is excerpted from Evaluation of the DC Opportunity Scholarship Program: Impacts After Three Years, *a report prepared by Wolf and his colleagues for the Institute of Education Sciences, which followed students in Washington, D.C., who were participating in the nation's first federally funded school choice/ voucher program. With few exceptions, there has been no improvement in academic achievement among students who chose their own schools, maintain Wolf et al. Parents, however, reported the belief that schools they picked were safer than the previous schools their children attended.*

Patrick Wolf et al., "Evaluation of the DC Oppprtunity Scholarship Program," Evaluation of the DC Opportunity Scholarship Program: Impacts After Three Years (NCEE 2009-4050), National Center for Education Evaluation and Regional Assistance, Institute of Education Sciences, U.S. Department of Education, 2009, pp. 31–51.

As you read, consider the following questions:

1. According to Wolf et al., what has a closer examination of the data from the first two years of the study revealed about the apparent achievement gains in reading and math?

2. Which subgroups of students were found to have no statistically significant improvements in reading, as cited by Wolf and his colleagues?

3. In the report, what advantages did parents of students who received opportunity scholarships find in the schools they chose for their children?

The statute that authorized the District of Columbia Opportunity Scholarship Program (OSP) mandated that the program be evaluated with regard to its impact on student test scores and safety, as well as the "success" of the program, which, in the design of this study, includes satisfaction with school choices. This chapter presents the impacts of the program on these outcomes 3 years after families and students applied to the OSP, or approximately 30 months after the start of their first school year in the program. . . .

The evaluation of the impact of the OSP is a longitudinal study, in that it tracks the outcomes of students over multiple years of their potential participation in the scholarship program. Two earlier reports described impacts 1 and 2 years after students applied to the OSP and were randomly assigned by lottery to either the treatment or control group. The results from those analyses indicated:

- In neither year were there statistically significant impacts on academic achievement overall or for students from SINI [schools identified as in need of improvement] schools, the key student subgroup defined in the law.

- In both year 1 and year 2, initial estimates suggested there were positive achievement impacts for several other subgroups. In year 1, the subgroup impacts were in math achievement, while in year 2 the impacts were in reading achievement. In both years, those impact estimates lost their statistical significance when adjustments for multiple comparisons were made, and thus the subgroup findings may have been "false discoveries."

- There were no impacts in year 1 or year 2 on either reading or math achievement for students in other subgroups, including those who were lower performing at application, males or females separately, students entering grades K–8 or high school, or students who applied to the program the second year (cohort 2).

- In both years, the program had a positive impact on parents' satisfaction with their child's school and parents' perceptions of school safety.

- In year 1 and year 2, students with OSP scholarships did not report being more satisfied with school or feeling safer than those without access to scholarships; in year 2 the program seemed to have a negative impact on school satisfaction for students with lower academic performance when they applied to the OSP, though adjustments for multiple comparisons suggest that could have been a false discovery.

- This same pattern of findings holds for the impact of *using* a scholarship as well as being *offered* a scholarship.

These were the results of the analysis of data collected 1 and 2 years after random assignment. The results presented in the remainder of this report are based on data collected 3 years after random assignment and about 30 months into any new educational experiences that may have been induced by the scholarship offer.

Year 3 Impacts on Student Achievement

The statute clearly identifies students' academic achievement as the primary outcome to be measured as part of the evaluation. This emphasis is consistent with the priority Congress placed on having the OSP serve students from low-performing schools. Academic achievement as a measure of program success is also well aligned with parents' stated priorities in choosing schools.

In summary, the analysis revealed:

- Positive and statistically significant impacts of the program on overall student achievement in reading after 3 years.

- No significant impacts on overall student achievement in math after 3 years.

- No significant achievement impacts in reading or math for students who came from SINI schools, the subgroup of students for whom the statute gave top priority.

- Positive programmatic impacts in reading achievement for 5 of the 10 subgroups examined: participants who applied from non-SINI schools, those who applied to the program with relatively higher levels of academic performance, female students, students entering grades K–8 at the time of application, and students from the first cohort of applicants [students who applied to the program the first year]. However, the positive subgroup reading impacts for female students and the first cohort of applicants should be interpreted with caution, as reliability tests for multiple comparison adjustments suggest that they could be false discoveries.

• No statistically significant test score differences in math between the treatment and control groups for any of the 10 subgroups of students. . . .

The statistical significance of impacts for particular subgroups of students in year 3 are consistent with those for students overall in math but not in reading. There were no impacts on math achievement for any of the 10 subgroups examined, as was true for the full impact sample. The offer of a scholarship, and therefore the use of a scholarship, had a statistically significant positive impact on reading achievement in the third year for half of the student subgroups, including at least two subgroups who applied with a relative advantage in academic preparation. The subgroups with positive reading impacts include:

• Students in the treatment group who had attended non-SINI public schools prior to the program, who scored an average of 6.6 scale score points higher in reading than students in the control group from non-SINI schools.

• Students in the treatment group who entered the program in the higher two-thirds of the applicant test-score performance distribution—averaging a 43 National Percentile Rank in reading at baseline—who scored an average of 5.5 scale score points higher in reading than students in the control group who applied to the OSP in the higher two-thirds of the test-score distribution.

• Female students in the treatment group, who scored an average of 5.1 scale score points higher in reading than females in the control group.

- Students in the treatment group who entered the program in grades K–8, who scored an average of 5.2 scale score points higher in reading than students in the control group who applied to the OSP entering grades K–8.

- Students in the treatment group from the first cohort of applicants, who scored an average of 8.7 scale score points higher in reading than students in the control group from cohort 1. . . .

There was no statistically significant subgroup impact in reading for students who applied from a school designated SINI between 2003 and 2005—the highest service priority for the program according to the statute. The analysis also did not show subgroup impacts for students who entered the program in the lower one-third of the applicant test-score performance distribution, male students, students who entered the program from high school, and cohort 2 students. . . .

Parents Report on School Safety

Overall, the parents of students offered an Opportunity Scholarship in the lottery subsequently reported their child's school to be safer and more orderly than did the parents of students in the control group. . . .

This impact of the offer of a scholarship on parental perceptions of safety and an orderly school climate was consistent across all subgroups of students examined, including parents of students from SINI and non-SINI schools, parents of students who entered the program with relatively higher and lower levels of academic achievement, parents of male and female students, parents of students in grades K–8 and 9–12, and parents of both cohort 1 and cohort 2. All of these subgroup impacts on parental views of school safety remained statistically significant after adjustments to account for multiple comparisons. The overall impact of the program, as well as the impacts for 9 of the 10 subgroups, was robust to both sensitivity tests. The exception was the impact of the program on parents of cohort 1 students, which lost statistical significance in the sensitivity test using the trimmed sample. . . .

Student Self-Report on School Safety

The students in grades 4–12 who completed surveys paint a different picture about school safety at their school than do their parents. The student index of school climate and safety asked students if they personally had been a victim of theft, drug-dealing, assaults, threats, bullying, or taunting or had observed weapons at school. On average, reports of school climate and safety by students offered scholarships through the lottery were not statistically different from those of the control group. That is, there was no evidence of an impact from the offer of a scholarship or the use of a scholarship on students' reports. No statistically significant findings were evident across the subgroups analyzed. Nor did the sensitivity tests conducted lead to a different set of overall findings.

Summary of Findings

This chapter presents the estimated impacts of the OSP 3 years after the initial random assignment of students to treatment or control groups. The evidence indicates that the treatment—*the offer* of a scholarship—generated a positive and statistically significant impact on the average reading test scores of the students in the study. The size of the overall reading impact is 3.1 months of additional schooling for the offer of the scholarship and 3.7 months of additional schooling for the use of a scholarship. Five of the 10 student subgroups examined demonstrated statistically significant reading impacts, with the positive impacts on the reading scores of SINI-never, higher baseline performing, and K-8 applicants retaining significance after adjustments for multiple comparisons. The highest priority subgroup—SINI-ever students—did not experience statistically significant achievement impacts from the offer or use of an OSP scholarship. No statistically significant treatment impacts were observed in math, overall or for any of the 10 student subgroups.

Overall, parents in the treatment group continued to perceive their child's school to be safer and were more likely to assign it a high grade compared to parents of the control group. The subgroup impacts were consistent with the overall estimates for school satisfaction, but 3 of the 10 parent groups—those of students who were more academically challenged (that is, students from SINI-ever schools or students in the lower one-third of the test-score distribution) or entering the slot-constrained high school grades when they applied to the program—did not report being more satisfied with their child's school if they were offered an Opportunity Scholarship.

As in the year 1 and year 2 impact reports released previously, student perceptions of school safety and satisfaction differed significantly from those of their parents in year 3. Student reports of school safety and climate and their likelihood of grading their school A or B were statistically indistinguishable between the treatment and control groups—overall and for all 10 student subgroups.

VIEWPOINT

"Many of the women in tenured senior positions found themselves effectively 'invisible' and 'marginalized' within their departments and excluded from participating in significant decisions."

Removing Bias in Academic Science and Engineering Will Narrow Gender Barriers

Committee on Maximizing the Potential of Women in Academic Science and Engineering

The Committee on Maximizing the Potential of Women in Academic Science and Engineering was formed by the members of the National Academies to investigate the gender imbalance in science and make recommendations for achieving better representation of women in university tenure and research positions. The following excerpt from the committee's book Beyond Bias and Barriers: Fulfilling the Potential of Women in Academic Science and Engineering *reviews some of the legislative strategies to help women advance professionally in the sciences and suggests ways that universities and research institutions can*

Committee on Maximizing the Potential of Women in Academic Science and Engineering, "Institutional Constraints," Beyond Bias and Barriers: Fulfilling the Potential of Women in Academic Science and Engineering, 2007, pp. 180–203. Reprinted with permission from the National Academies Press, Washington, DC. Copyright © 2007 by the National Academy of Sciences. All rights reserved.

make small changes in their systems that enable women to more effectively participate so they can achieve at the same rate as men.

As you read, consider the following questions:

1. According to the viewpoint authors, at what percentage of female representation within a department do gender issues and hiring inequalities seem to disappear?

2. What are three examples of government legislation that were passed to prevent the systematic discrimination against women in the workplace?

3. What is one example of an "invisible" feature of culture within a professional organization that was inadvertently harming women, as cited by the authors?

The obstacles and impediments that women scientists and engineers experience as they pursue careers in academic institutions do not arise solely from institutional constraints, stereotyping, or bias. Organizational studies show that introducing members of previously excluded groups into social units creates predictable attitudes and reactions among both the new arrivals and the established group members. The exact nature of these behaviors depends in part on the personalities and attitudes of the established members and on the number of newcomers relative to the group at large. Sometimes the members engage in bullying or threatening behavior, at other times, welcoming and supportive behavior. The reactions evolve as the proportion changes.

Bullying behavior is often systematically applied to women and can persist even in the highest levels of the academic hierarchy. Bullying is an abuse or misuse of power characterized by work-oriented aggression and is distinct from sexual harassment in nature and target of the aggression. Work-related bullying may involve excessive assignment of work, reassignment of responsibilities, unfair criticism, and excessive monitoring. Bullies tend to target newcomers, particularly those from groups not well represented in the workplace. In science and engineering academic environments, this means women are often targeted. Furthermore, gender plays a role in the form and perception of bullying. So, although both men and women are bullied, women tend to be affected differently. The combined effects of being more likely to be targeted, less likely to report bullying behavior, and lacking support structures can translate to a hostile environment for women in high academic and administrative positions. Mentoring programs have been effective at strengthening the support infrastructure and helping women faculty survive and overcome bullying. Ombuds offices are another avenue providing advocacy and support for those targeted.

For the small numbers of women in faculty and leadership positions in science and engineering a major issue is singularity or tokenism. Numerical representation is an influential structural characteristic of most work organizations. Minority group size affects attitudes, achievement, and the frequency and quantity of interpersonal contact between majority and minority group members and may also affect salaries. However, the reliance on quotas to eliminate the occupational inequalities faced by tokens, the "add women and minority group members and stir" model, may hinder the integration of the workplace if the underlying institutional structures are not addressed.

Pioneers and Tipping Points

Pioneering women scientists and engineers who are among the first of their sex to enter a field or laboratory or to be hired in a department face the predictable problems of tokenism and scarcity, including social isolation and extreme visibility. The problems are more pronounced for pioneering women who belong to underrepresented racial or ethnic minorities. Thus, even when women scientists and engineers achieve high academic rank in Research I universities, full equality with their male colleagues often eludes them.

A survey of women science faculty members at MIT [Massachusetts Institute of Technology], for example, found that those in junior positions felt that their departments supported them and that gender bias would not threaten their future careers. Many of the women in tenured senior positions found themselves effectively "invisible" and "marginalized" within their departments and excluded from participating in significant decisions. Even more striking, those extremely accomplished scientists reported that their sense of marginalization had grown as their careers advanced. Early in their careers, they, like their junior colleagues of today, had believed "that gender discrimination was 'solved' in the previous generation and would not touch them. Gradually, however, their eyes were opened to the realization that the playing field was not level after all."

If the number of women in a field or department grows to about 20% of total membership, a "critical mass" develops, and a social tipping point occurs. Women now form a noticeable contingent in the organization and start to perceive their common interests, joining together to press for improvements in policies relevant to their needs, such as those concerning family issues. They also begin to appear in leadership positions. With these signs of solidarity, however, the first signs of backlash begin to appear among the men, who start to perceive women as a threat to the established order and to their traditional position and privileges. Men may begin to resist further hiring or promotion of women, sometimes overtly but often covertly.

If female representation continues to increase and reaches 40%–60% of the group, a second tipping point occurs. Now gender issues seem to matter less and attract less attention. Such issues as bias and inequality in hiring, pay and promotion seem to disappear. If the proportion of women continues

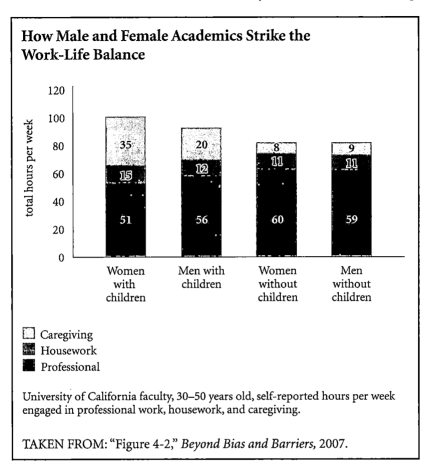

How Male and Female Academics Strike the Work-Life Balance

Caregiving
Housework
Professional

University of California faculty, 30–50 years old, self-reported hours per week engaged in professional work, housework, and caregiving.

TAKEN FROM: "Figure 4-2," *Beyond Bias and Barriers*, 2007.

to grow, however, a third tipping point occurs; at 90% gender segregation returns; the department or field is now perceived as female and therefore less appropriate to men. The changeover from male to female can bring substantial consequences, in that fields viewed as female are less prestigious and poorer paying than those viewed as male.

Legal Approaches to Discrimination

The need for universities to develop practices that provide women scientists and engineers an equal chance of career success is far more than a moral imperative. Under modern antidiscrimination law, it is also a legal requirement. The low representation of women in the upper reaches of academe was long attributed to the "chilly climate" of those high realms. Today, however, legal thinkers argue that remedial action must go beyond vague formulations of creating a culture of faculty support. Universities must meet their obligation as employers to provide a workplace free of unlawful discrimination. . . .

The numbers of women earning bachelor's and graduate degrees have increased, but in many fields of science and engineering, an increasing PhD pool has not necessarily led to increased representation of women on faculties. What legal options exist to redress this situation? Some have argued for using the federal Title IX statute to compel science and engineering departments to hire women by threatening to withhold federal funding from institutions that fail to do so. That strategy has worked well to increase the number and accessibility of athletic programs for women. . . .

Effective use of both Title IX and Title VI is critical for women—and especially women of color—in science and engineering fields. In addition, Title VII of the Civil Rights Act of 1964 prohibits employment discrimination based on race, color, religion, sex, or national origin in any organization with more than 15 employees. It bars discrimination from recruitment through termination, and it has been used in most tenure denial cases. Even though Title VII was originally intended to protect racial minorities from employment discrimination, it appears to have been more effective in remedying sex segregation. The Equal Pay Act of 1963 bars sex-based wage differentials between people who do the same or substantially similar jobs. Executive Order 11246 requires all federal contractors to file a discrimination statement and affirmative action plans. The Family and Medical Leave Act applies to all workplaces with 50 or more employees and guarantees an employee 12 weeks per year of unpaid leave to care for a family member. Title IX, passed in 1972, prohibits sex-based discrimination in or exclusion from any educational program or activity receiving federal financial assistance. Finally, constitutional standards of equal protection apply, but only for public organizations.

Traditionally, proving discrimination involved comparing a plaintiff—for example, a woman denied tenure who claimed to be the subject of discrimination—with a similarly situated person in the other group. Recent cases, however, have opened a promising new approach by finding that the existence of stereotyping can serve as proof of discrimination. Thus, a woman caught under the glass ceiling for purportedly being "too aggressive" to be a collegial colleague, or one up against the maternal wall for "lacking dedication" to her career because she sought to reduce her hours during her child's infancy may have grounds for a suit.

Those legal trends can encourage institutions not only to take steps to reduce stereotyping but also to provide services and establish programs that meet federal requirements and remove constraints that limit faculty (usually women) who have caretaking responsibilities. One-third of academic institutions, for example, have family policies that appear to violate the Pregnancy Discrimination Act, which forbids treating pregnancy differently from other temporary disabilities. Women— and, in some cases, men—academics who try to assert their rights under such laws as the Family and Medical Leave Act, which mandates 12 weeks of unpaid leave and the right to return to work, however, often find themselves pressured to return sooner than they wish and face increased scrutiny, adverse career consequences, and other forms of retribution.

The odds in sex discrimination cases do not favor plaintiffs. In most sex discrimination cases that reach trial, universities win. Most cases never reach trial, however, because they are dropped or resolved during the litigation process. A report by the American Association of University Women [AAUW] revealed that women academics won only a minority of lawsuits alleging improper denial of tenure. Bringing such a case usually entails substantial effort and financial risk and the possibility of being considered a troublemaker. "It taints all levels of your professional life at the university," according to a woman who sued and ultimately settled with the university. . . .

Effecting Institutional Change—Incrementally

Transforming academic institutions so that they will foster the career advancement of women scientists and engineers is a complex task. The NSF's [National Science Foundation's] AD-VANCE program is geared specifically to promote such institutional transformation. It reflects the increasing understanding that individual accommodations and help are not sufficient to bring gender equity to the academy; long-standing sector-wide measures appear to be necessary to accomplish the integration of women into the academy. . . .

A number of organizations have successfully fostered female employees' career advancement by undertaking experiments that produce small but important changes in work procedures, practices, or norms. In most organizations in which women's advancement and leadership opportunities have been limited, the problem is not old-style, overt sex discrimination, but rather unrecognized features of the organizational culture that affect men and women differently. Those features tend to be so embedded in organizational life as to be invisible. They generally also bear no obvious relationship to gender. The only indication that such issues exist may be an unexplained inability of the organization to attract, retain, or promote women in sufficient numbers despite an apparent willingness to do so.

In an approach to overcoming such problems called small-win experiments, members of the organization, preferably with the backing of leadership, systematically seek out the features and set about finding ways to change them. An example of such a constraining cultural feature in one organization was a looseness about punctuality and the length of meetings that made it difficult for many women—who often live with tighter time restrictions than men because of their family responsibilities—to attend all the meetings they needed to attend to keep abreast of developments in the organization. Overtly establishing a new norm that meetings start and end at the announced times is a small-win experiment that made the organization much more congenial to women. In another example, the custom of giving major credit for a successful project to the lead scientist devalued the "invisible work" of other professionals and support staff, many of whom were women. The solution was to establish a way to give public recognition to the importance of "invisible work" and the people who do it.

Successful small-win experiments must be carefully tailored to the specific circumstances of a particular organization. That requires a close examination of the organization's culture to uncover unstated assumptions about what constitutes success and who attains it, as well as implicit norms about how work is done and recognition granted. The consequences of the assumptions and practices must also be examined, and then discrete, concrete ways of changing the ones that adversely affect women must be devised. Once the project is under way, however, "it's surprising how quickly people can come up with ideas for small wins—and how quickly they can be put into action." . . .

In addition to examining the campus climate, it is important that the university leadership make it known that it is committed to the advancement of women and minority groups. This may include drawing attention to the status of women, demonstrating that the inferior status of women is a problem for the entire university, noting that the campus has zero tolerance for sexual harassment and discrimination, and making deans and department heads accountable for what happens to women in their constituencies.

VIEWPOINT

> "Females show far less interest than
> males on the mechanical, military, and
> athletic scales, and somewhat less on
> the math and science scales."

Enforcing Title IX Will Not Narrow the Gender Achievement Gap in the Sciences

Patricia Hausman

Patricia Hausman is a behavioral scientist and a former editor of NAS Science Insights. *The following viewpoint appeared on the Web site of the National Association of Scholars. It is a response to a report titled* Beyond Bias and Barriers: Fulfilling the Potential of Women in Academic Science and Engineering *and the subsequent congressional hearing about applying Title IX regulations to university science programs. Hausman identifies errors and assumptions within the report and describes the possible negative, unintended consequences of government interference in the gender balance of science and engineering departments.*

Patricia Hausman, "Feminizing Science: The Alchemy of Title IX," *Academic Questions*, vol. 21, Fall 2008. Journal of the National Association of Scholar, published by Springer (www.springerlink.com). Copyright © 2008 National Association of Scholars. All rights reserved. Reproduced by permission of the author.

As you read, consider the following questions:

1. According to Hausman, what statistics regarding new doctorates and the award of tenure-track positions to females in the math and sciences undermine claims of sexism against women in those fields?

2. How could the enforcement of Title IX legislation for the sciences negatively affect women who are already working as scientists at universities, as described by Hausman?

3. According to the viewpoint author, how do males' and females' scores on the Strong Interest Inventory and Study of Values assessment tests suggest a reasonable disproportion of women in certain science, engineering, or mathematics careers?

The physical sciences have long resisted most inanities of the postmodern university. Nonetheless, these disciplines have not rejected all foolish notions prevalent on campus today. For some time, departments of physical sciences, engineering, and mathematics (SEM) have accepted feminist contentions that their practices are responsible for the underrepresentation of women in their ranks. Efforts to reverse this situation have followed—from female-friendly admissions standards to special dorms designed to support female engineering students.

These efforts have failed to produce parity of the sexes in SEM fields—a predictable outcome given that their underlying premise is false. As their failure to deliver desired effects has become clear, proponents have rarely reconsidered their beliefs as to why female underrepresentation persists. Rather, talk has turned to use of coercive methods to augment current efforts. This thinking has been inspired by the use—or more accurately, abuse—of Title IX of the 1972 Federal Education Amendments to force proportional representation of women in college sports.

Beyond Bias and Barriers: Fulfilling the Potential of Women in Academic Science and Engineering is perhaps the best example of this move toward coercive approaches. Published by the National Academy of Sciences, this report is the work of its Committee on Maximizing the Potential of Women in Academic Science and Engineering. The committee was asked to

- review and assess the research on gender issues in science and engineering, including innate differences in cognition, implicit bias, and faculty diversity; and

- examine the institutional culture and practices in academic institutions that contribute to and discourage talented individuals from realizing their full potential as scientists and engineers.

Obviously, this charge was uncharacteristic of scientific work, for it instructed the committee to *assume* that enough institutional factors are responsible for female underrepresentation to warrant an Academy report. An objective analysis would make no such assumption—nor rule out the possibility that some institutional practices actually favor females. . . .

Statistics Belie Purported Bias

Beyond Bias and Barriers is a report in the woe-is-me tradition of "gender equity" literature. Its authors see female scientists as hapless victims of an academic world created of, by, and for men. To them, university science is rife with obstacles that obstruct the paths of women, preventing them from fulfilling their potential.

It is a curious plaint. By their very nature, scientists and engineers are among the most objective individuals in the population—if not *the* most objective. This does not render them immune from bias. However, one should take due care before accusing scientists of sexism. This is a venue where someone may demand supporting evidence. The kind that can withstand true scientific scrutiny.

It is remarkable how poorly the committee fares on this count. Its executive summary asserts, "Women are very likely to face discrimination in every field of science and engineering." Yet, hard data to support this claim prove elusive. As the report progresses, it reveals that female physicists earned 13 percent of new doctorates in 2004, yet were awarded 18 percent of new junior faculty positions. In math, the figures were 31 and 28 percent, respectively. No data are provided for engineers. However, the American Society for Engineering Education reported in 2005 that 17 percent of tenure/tenure-track assistant professors were female. Women earned 17 to 18 percent of the engineering doctorates in the preceding five-year period. The suggestion that sex discrimination is routine is not easily reconciled with these numbers.

The tenure data are no less striking. Although women in the physical sciences are 1 to 3 percent less likely than men to become tenured, those in the life sciences and engineering are 2 to 4 percent *more likely* than males to achieve this milestone. Further, the committee fails to disclose that, depending on the type of institution, female scientists are two to five times as likely as males to obtain early tenure.

Given these facts, one might think that feminists would be beaming with pride about the success of female scientists. Not those on this committee. They want a major effort by federal agencies, Congress, foundations, and professional societies to slay the gender inequity monster that, in their view, still does his misogynistic best to prevent advancement of women in academic SEM. . . .

Applying Title IX to the Sciences

Most chapters of the report include recommendations for increasing the participation of women in SEM, particularly in the university. Some are useful, such as the suggestion that institutions revisit policies regarding dual-career couples. Others make no sense—among them the call for paid parental leave for graduate and postdoctoral students, as well as coverage of child care and elder care expenses when scientists travel. That the absence of these benefits affects women's participation in SEM is doubtful; many fields lack such perks yet are almost exclusively female.

Of all the recommendations, one merits particular scrutiny. It is the call for creation of a "gender equity" bureaucracy involving the federal government, professional societies, and an interinstitutional compliance agency. Working in concert, these players would set "gender equity" standards for SEM, collect data, monitor universities for compliance, and impose penalties for violations.

Accepting a burdensome regulatory regime absent data justifying such intervention would set a terrible precedent. Such endorsement would reinforce beliefs that discrimination and "barriers" explain the underrepresentation of women in SEM. Research from the university itself shows this notion to be untenable. For the university to acquiesce to regulation that presumes the existence of widespread discrimination therefore would be tantamount to proclaiming that the truth does not matter. Moreover, the proposed regulatory scheme envisions use of Title IX. This should concern every member of the faculty.

The committee gives little insight into how it would apply Title IX to the academic sciences. It simply includes a slightly modified version of the "three-prong" compliance test that has had devastating effects on male college sports. Under the committee's version of the test, universities must do one of the following:

- provide participation opportunities substantially proportional to the ratio of males to females in the student body

- show a history and continuing practice of upgrading girls' and women's programs

- meet the interests and abilities of women on campus

The committee does not say whether it would apply these mandates on a department-by-department basis or to the combined enrollment of all SEM disciplines. Though the latter would be less burdensome than the former, either scenario would be disastrous.

The first option would presumably require the proportion of males and females "substantially" to match their overall enrollment. It reflects a conviction that the sexes have or should have identical interests, and as a consequence, deviations from proportional representation indicate discrimination. As will be discussed shortly, an entire subdiscipline in psychology refutes this tenaciously held belief.

In some fields of science—physics and engineering, for example—males often outnumber female students by 4:1 (and sometimes more). It is unlikely that departments with such lopsided enrollments could approach a 1:1 ratio simply by adding female students. Even if cost were no object, finding sufficient numbers of qualified and interested females would be a daunting challenge. Accordingly, achieving proportionality would almost certainly require the exclusion of men— regardless of how well qualified—just as application of Title IX's bizarre concept of equality to athletics has caused the elimination of more than three hundred male teams.

Although proportionality is the "gold standard" for demonstrating compliance with Title IX, a university could opt for another method if unable to achieve it. The first alternative is compliance through "upgrading women's programs." This may be workable in college athletics because the sexes play on separate teams. But they are not separate in the classroom, nor is it necessary for them to be. In fact, it is difficult to imagine anything more counterproductive than special science programs for females. Such programs would merely reinvigorate arguments that women cannot succeed in "real" science classes. Thus, it appears that this option is not viable and that the committee failed to consider whether a standard designed for sex-segregated situations makes sense for coeducational ones.

The other alternative permitted when proportionality is not possible—"meet[ing] the interests and abilities of women on campus"—implies a right for any interested female on campus to be accommodated if she meets certain standards. A university seeking to comply under this option would presumably have to set minimum qualifications that, in its experience, predict a good chance of completing its SEM programs.

Such a mandate should set off alarm bells throughout academic SEM. American science has not taken its preeminent position in the world by accepting those who meet minimum standards. It owes its success to a tradition of seeking the best and brightest. Moreover, the notion that an academic institution is obliged to accommodate every female on campus who meets minimum qualifications takes the quota mentality to a new level. It would confer a right to enter a campus SEM program regardless of where one was initially admitted. Granting female students special rights to academic accommodation sounds like a recipe for endless litigation. It is also unlikely to create an atmosphere of mutual respect.

Oddly enough, female faculty (as well as male) could end up the big losers if Title IX is applied to academic SEM. The penalty for noncompliance is applied university-wide. The committee opines that loss of all federal funding, as provided for by law, is excessive. As an alternative it suggests "withdrawal of an institution's ability to compete for federal funds for a given period." If imposed, an institution's female (and male) scientists would lose their right to seek federal funds for the prescribed time period. The committee does not explain why they should be penalized for what is beyond their control. Other potential losers include some of the women seeking careers in such fields as veterinary medicine, optometry, and pharmacy. After all, men pushed out of SEM have to go somewhere. One can reasonably expect some to choose other scientific fields, increasing competition for places that women hope to earn.

The report does not consider such impacts, nor stop with Title IX. It mentions an Executive Order and other laws that the committee sees as useful for addressing "inequities" in SEM. One shudders to think where all of this could lead. The *New York Times* recently reported that Title IX "compliance reviews" now being performed by federal agencies include "taking inventories of lab space and interviewing faculty members and students in physics and engineering departments" at selected universities.

The potential for unintended consequences from imposing Title IX on academic science is obvious, but its magnitude is difficult to predict. The regulations have succeeded in dramatically reshaping athletics because students are easily classified as athletes or nonathletes. Degree completion is more complex. Rules may be used to deny males the right to major in computer science, but can the law stop them from majoring in English and taking the equivalent of such a major as electives? If not, what purpose would be served? The regulated have a long history of figuring out how to circumvent the silliness of regulators. One cannot rule out the possibility that they will ultimately find ways to turn a gender quota bureaucracy on its head.

Males and Females Are Interested in Different Things

The Committee asserts: "[I]t is not poor high school preparation, ability, or effort, but rather the educational climate of science and engineering departments that correlates with the

Women Seeking Faculty Positions

To investigate possible gender bias in university hiring, Congress commissioned the "Gender Differences at Critical Transitions" report, published in June [2009] by the National Academy of Sciences. The study highlighted some gender disparities but also noted that women are being hired at faster rates than men for university jobs in some high-tech fields.

	Biology	Chemistry	Civil Engineering	Electrical Engineering	Mathematics	Physics
Ph.D.s who are women	45%	32%	18%	12%	25%	14%
Tenure-track job applicants who are women	26	18	16	11	20	12
Tenure-track job offers that go to women	34	29	32	32	32	20

TAKEN FROM: Neil Munro, "Science Faces Title IX Test," *National Journal Magazine*, July 4, 2009.

high proportion of undergraduates who opt out of science and engineering." To the contrary, research from the field of vocational psychology demonstrates that the primary factors in career choice are not external, but internal. One can think of them as a function of personality.

The aspects of personality that best explain career choice are represented in assessment tools designed to help individuals determine the occupations best for them. Two of these are the Strong Interest Inventory and the Study of Values. Each scores an individual's career interests based on six *themes* or *dimensions*. On the former, the largest sex difference is on the *realistic* theme, where males far outscore females. Males also score higher on the *investigative* theme, but the difference is considerably smaller. On the Study of Values, the largest sex difference is on the *theoretical* dimension, with the average male outscoring the average female. These differences do much to explain female underrepresentation in certain SEM fields. Women are most underrepresented in scientific occupations classified as investigative-realistic and known to attract those with a strong theoretical bent.

The Strong Interest Inventory also includes Basic Interest Scales. Females show far less interest than males on the mechanical, military, and athletic scales, and somewhat less on the math and science scales. Thus, Title IX activists are ironically determined to increase the participation of women in two of the three areas where they express the least enthusiasm. It is fair to ask why.

Attempting to lure capable women into SEM fields incompatible with their interest profiles does them a disservice. For those bound by the American Psychological Association Code of Ethics, it would be of questionable compliance with the obligation to practice consistent with scientific principles and avoid harm to clients and patients. Being part of a demographic group that has achieved equal participation with another group has never been shown to predict career satisfaction and success. What predicts a good outcome is an occupation consistent with one's interests, values, abilities, and skills. . . .

The essential point is absolutely not that females lack the ability to succeed at the highest levels of SEM. It is that fewer women than men have the cognitive pattern associated with such success. This is especially true for fields where mental rotation and mechanical abilities are critical, as far more males than females are gifted in these domains. Pretending that these differences do not exist will not make them disappear, for all are rooted in human biology. Their interaction with the differences in interests described earlier produces the underrepresentation of women in SEM that feminists (and others) erroneously attribute to discrimination.

Periodical Bibliography

The following articles have been selected to supplement the diverse views presented in this chapter.

Anita L. Allen   "Paid to Achieve: Do Families Need Cash Incentives?" *Star-Ledger* (Newark, NJ), June 24, 2007.

Sharon Anderson et al.   "Which Achievement Gap?" *Phi Delta Kappan*, March 2007.

Nanette Asimov   "Summit Called to Address Racial Disparities in Academic Performance," *San Francisco Chronicle*, November 12, 2007.

Kevin Carey and   "School Funding's Tragic Flaw," Center on Re-
Marguerite Roza   inventing Public Education, May 2008.

Sam Dillon   "'No Child' Law Is Not Closing a Racial Gap," *New York Times*, April 29, 2009.

Danna Ethan and   "Promoting Healthy Vision in Students:
Charles E. Basch   Progress and Challenges in Policy, Programs, and Research," *Journal of School Health*, August 2008.

Walt Gardner   "Do Better Schools Help the Poor?" *Christian Science Monitor*, July 17, 2008.

Jay P. Greene   "The Odd Couple: Murray and Rothstein Find Some Unexpected Common Ground," *Education Next*, Fall 2007.

Frederick M. Hess and   "NCLB and the Competitiveness Agenda:
Andrew J. Rotherham   Happy Collaboration or a Collision Course?" *Phi Delta Kappan*, January 2007.

Haifeng "Charlie"   "Mapping Academic Achievement and Public
Zhang and David J.   School Choice Under the No Child Left Behind
Cowen   Legislation," *Southeastern Geographer*, March 22, 2009.

For Further Discussion

Chapter 1

1. Students can be placed in many different kinds of groups, such as racial identification or family income level. Educators and administrators often look at these groups to identify problems and determine solutions for improving academic achievement, attendance, test scores, discipline, and more. Is it reasonable to assess and correct groups rather than individuals? Are students with like attributes (for example, living in single-parent households) so similar that they benefit from the same interventions?

2. Students rely on their families as much as their teachers and counselors for information about succeeding in school and pursuing higher education. Are parents, siblings, and other relatives with college experience better resources than school professionals? Even if all parents and students can easily access the same amount of information about college admissions and scholarships, do students from families with a history of college attendance have a significant edge on students who will be the first people in their families to attend?

3. If, as Frances Spielhagen argues, the mathematics achievement gap could be narrowed or closed by having more students take eighth-grade algebra, why aren't more eighth-grade pre-algebra classes turned into algebra classes by schools and districts? If, as Alfinio Flores argues, white students tend to have better access to highly skilled math teachers, why aren't teachers serving low-achieving or minority populations given better training? What practical or

financial considerations might prevent schools from
implementing these suggested changes to math education
departments?

Chapter 2

1. Jean Yonemura Wing and Jamie Lew emphasize the extent
   to which a student's family background affects how well
   he or she is able to use his or her school time and resources. In your experience, do counselors and teachers
   favor students who already know what questions to ask?
   Should counselors be more sympathetic to students without these cultural and family advantages or should they
   give most of their attention to students who actively seek
   out help?

2. Joel I. Klein and Steve Giegerich describe at length some
   of the unique problems that plague urban schools—especially poor ones—and affect student achievement. Are
   school and neighborhood violence and poor teachers
   separate problems or are they linked to each other? Would
   eliminating violence eventually result in better teachers?

Chapter 3

1. Do low-achieving and high-achieving students benefit differently from arts and technology programs? Should
   schools worrying about the achievement gap focus on the
   core subjects—math, science, English—more than on
   supplemental subjects?

Chapter 4

1. According to Naomi Chudowsky and her coauthors, the
   No Child Left Behind (NCLB) Act is reducing the
   achievement gap nationwide by improving the standardized test scores of students at low-performing schools. Liz
   Hollingworth argues, however, that NCLB is harming

schools in ways that were never anticipated. Should the federal government have the power to judge and sanction schools? Should state governments? What are some benefits and drawbacks of making schools and school districts completely responsible for their successes or failures? What are some benefits and drawbacks of national standards for student knowledge and performance?

2. Title IX legislation was passed in 1972 to ensure that girls had equal access to educational activities that were formerly considered the province of boys. The achievement gap between boys and girls in math and science has radically narrowed in the decades since, although the gap in the number of men and women working in the sciences has not changed as much. What reasons might prevent adult women from making the same professional gains in math and science that men do?

Organizations to Contact

The editors have compiled the following list of organizations concerned with the issues debated in this book. The descriptions are derived from materials provided by the organizations. All have publications or information available for interested readers. The list was compiled on the date of publication of the present volume; the information provided here may change. Be aware that many organizations take several weeks or longer to respond to inquiries, so allow as much time as possible.

Advancement Via Individual Determination (AVID)
9246 Lightwave Avenue, Suite 200, San Diego, CA 92123
(858) 380-4800 • fax: (858) 268-2265
Web site: www.avidonline.org

Advancement Via Individual Determination (AVID) is a fourth- through twelfth-grade system to prepare students in the academic middle for four-year college eligibility. These are largely low-income students who are capable of completing a college prep curriculum but are falling short of their potential. The core component is the AVID elective, which supports students as they tackle the most rigorous classes. AVID class curriculum is developed by secondary education teachers and college professors. It is supported with trained college students who volunteer as tutors and aides, enhanced with community speakers and special presentations, and extended to home with family programs and workshops. The Web site offers resources to help students prepare for college, financial aid, and entrance exams.

Association on Higher Education and Disability (AHEAD)
107 Commerce Center Drive, Suite 204
Huntersville, NC 28078
(704) 947-7779 • fax: (704) 948-7779
Web site: www.ahead.org

Association on Higher Education and Disability (AHEAD) is a professional membership organization for individuals involved in the development of policy and in the provision of quality services to meet the needs of persons with disabilities involved in all areas of higher education; it has members worldwide. It works specifically to train educators and administrators about the particular needs of disabled students and the issues faced by disabled students on college campuses. It hosts an annual international conference and publishes the scholarly *Journal of Postsecondary Education and Disability*, as well as the frequent *ALERT* electronic newsletter, which keeps members informed about current news and topics.

Bill & Melinda Gates Foundation

PO Box 23350, Seattle, WA   98102
(206) 709-3100
e-mail: info@gatesfoundation.org
Web site: www.gatesfoundation.org

The domestic arm of the Bill & Melinda Gates Foundation works to ensure greater opportunity for all Americans through the attainment of secondary and postsecondary education with genuine economic value. Its programs help students graduate from high school ready for success and prepared to earn postsecondary degrees, and it funds scholarships to help individual students. It also supports computer and Internet networks at public libraries, ensuring that every person has free public access. Special initiatives and advocacy efforts expand the reach of their educational philanthropy.

Expanding Your Horizons (EYH) Network

Mills College, 5000 MacArthur Boulevard
Oakland, CA   94613
(510) 430-2222 • fax: (510) 430-2090
Web site: www.expandingyourhorizons.org

The Expanding Your Horizons (EYH) Network is a nonprofit membership organization of educators, scientists, mathematicians, parents, community leaders, and government and corporate representatives. Its mission is to encourage young women to pursue science, technology, engineering, and mathematics (STEM) careers. EYH Network's programs provide STEM role models and hands-on activities for middle and high school girls. Its ultimate goal is to motivate girls to become innovative and creative thinkers ready to meet twenty-first century challenges. EYH Network's annual conferences are presented nationwide and feature hands-on activities and workshops to nurture girls' interests in science and math and introduce them to STEM professionals who could serve as mentors and role models.

Institute for Urban and Minority Education (IUME)

Teachers College, Columbia University, 525 West 120th Street
New York, NY 10027-6696
(212) 678-3413 • fax: (212) 678-4137
e-mail: iume@tc.columbia.edu
Web site: http://iume.tc.columbia.edu

For almost forty years, the Institute for Urban and Minority Education (IUME) has used advocacy, demonstration, evaluation, information dissemination, research, and technical assistance to study and seek to improve the quality of life chances through education in the communities of urban and minority peoples. Its efforts and initiatives are focused on increasing university and community partnerships to promote institutional services in the community as well as civic engagement and social responsibility. One such partnership is with the Children's Aid Society; together they formed the African American Male Initiative "Steps to Success" program.

National Association of State Directors of Migrant Education (NASDME)

1001 Connecticut Avenue NW, Suite 915
Washington, DC 20036
Web site: www.nasdme.org

National Association of State Directors of Migrant Education (NASDME) is the professional organization of state officials charged with the administrative responsibilities of effectively and productively helping migrant children succeed in school. NASDME provides its members ongoing information about events and activities, and offers new members training, guidance, and counsel. It hosts the annual National Migrant Education Conference.

National Indian Education Association (NIEA)

110 Maryland Avenue NE, Suite 104, Washington, DC   20002
(202) 544-7290 • fax: (202) 544-7293
e-mail: niea@niea.org
Web site: www.niea.org

Incorporated in 1970, the National Indian Education Association (NIEA) is the largest and oldest Native American education organization in the United States and strives to keep native cultures moving toward educational equity. It is committed to increasing educational opportunities and resources for Native American, Alaska Native, and Native Hawaiian students while protecting their cultural and linguistic traditions. NIEA hosts a national convention annually, provides information about scholarships for Native American students of the United States, and serves as a political advocate for Native American education at the national level. Its quarterly publication, *NIEA News*, won the 2009 North American Indigenous Images Award for best magazine.

National Summer Learning Association

800 Wyman Park Drive, Suite 110, Baltimore, MD   21211
(410) 856-1370
Web site: www.summerlearning.org

The vision of the National Summer Learning Association is for every child to be safe, healthy, and engaged in learning during the summer. To realize that vision, its mission is to connect and equip schools and community organizations to deliver quality summer learning programs to the nation's youth to help close the achievement gap. The organization's efforts are focused on increasing the number of providers offering high-quality summer learning programs to young people living in poverty, increasing the number of organizations and policy makers that identify summer learning as a public policy priority, and increasing funding for high-quality summer learning programs for young people who currently lack choices and opportunities.

Office of Head Start (OHS)

Administration for Children and Families
1250 Maryland Avenue SW, 8th Floor, Washington, DC 20024
(202) 205-8572
Web site: www.acf.hhs.gov

The Head Start program provides grants to local agencies for comprehensive child development services to economically disadvantaged children and families, with a special focus on helping preschoolers develop the early reading and math skills they need to be successful in school. Head Start programs promote school readiness by enhancing the social and cognitive development of children through the provision of educational, health, nutritional, social, and other services to enrolled children and families. They engage parents in their children's learning and help them in making progress toward their educational, literacy, and employment goals. The Office of Head Start is part of the Administration for Children and Families, an arm of the U.S. Department of Health and Human Services.

United Nations Educational, Scientific and Cultural Organization (UNESCO)

7, Place de Fontenoy, Paris   75352
    France
+33 (0)1 45 68 10 00 • fax: +33 (0)1 45 67 16 90
e-mail: bpi@unesco.org
Web site: www.unesco.org

The United Nations Educational, Scientific and Cultural Organization's (UNESCO's) Education division leads the global Education for All (EFA) movement, which aims to meet the learning needs of all children, youth, and adults. Its goals are to expand early childhood care and education, provide free and compulsory primary education for all, promote learning and life skills for young people and adults, increase adult literacy by 50 percent, and improve the quality of education. UNESCO publishes a variety of reports, statistics, and research as well as the annual *Global Monitoring Report* on the movement's progress toward its goals.

United Negro College Fund (UNCF)
8260 Willow Oaks Corporate Drive, PO Box 10444
Fairfax, VA   22031-8044
(800) 331-2244
Web site: www.uncf.org

The United Negro College Fund (UNCF) first uttered the famous statement, "A mind is a terrible thing to waste." To close the educational attainment gap between African Americans and the majority population, UNCF helps promising students attend college and graduate by providing operating funds for its thirty-nine member colleges, making it possible for these institutions to reduce fees and make college more affordable to more students. It administers four hundred scholarship and internship programs and serves as a national advocate for minority higher education by representing the public policy interests of its students and member colleges. *An Evening of Stars* is its major annual fund-raising television program, but it sponsors smaller events throughout the nation at all times of year.

U.S. Department of Education (ED)
400 Maryland Avenue SW, Washington, DC   20202
(800) 872-5327
Web site: www.ed.gov

The U.S. Department of Education (ED) was created in 1980 to promote student achievement and preparation for global competitiveness by fostering educational excellence and ensuring equal access to education. The ED is the parent organization of the national No Child Left Behind (NCLB) Act and provides information about NCLB efforts in each state. It also runs the eight TRIO federal outreach and student services programs, which include, among others, Upward Bound, Upward Bound Math-Science, and Veterans Upward Bound. These programs are designed for students from low-income families or families in which neither parent holds a bachelor's degree to help these individuals achieve success from middle school through postsecondary level.

Bibliography of Books

William G.
Bowen, Matthew
M. Chingos, and
Michael S.
McPherson

Crossing the Finish Line: Completing College at America's Public Universities. Princeton, NJ: Princeton University Press, 2009.

Camille Z.
Charles et al.

Taming the River: Negotiating the Academic, Financial, and Social Currents in Selective Colleges and Universities. Princeton, NJ: Princeton University Press, 2009.

James P. Comer

What I Learned in School: Reflections on Race, Child Development, and School Reform. San Francisco, CA: Jossey-Bass, 2009.

Gilberto Q.
Conchas

The Color of Success: Race and High-Achieving Urban Youth. New York: Teachers College Press, 2006.

Lisa D. Delpit

Other People's Children: Cultural Conflict in the Classroom. New York: New Press, 2006.

Peter Demerath

Producing Success: The Culture of Personal Advancement in an American High School. Chicago, IL: University of Chicago Press, 2009.

Lise Eliot

Pink Brain, Blue Brain: How Small Differences Grow into Troublesome Gaps—and What We Can Do About It. Boston, MA: Houghton Mifflin Harcourt, 2009.

William A. Fischel   *Making the Grade: The Economic
                       Evolution of American School Districts.*
                       Chicago, IL: University of Chicago
                       Press, 2009.

Steven H.   *Billions of Drops in Millions of
Goldberg   Buckets: Why Philanthropy Doesn't
                       Advance Social Progress.* Hoboken, NJ:
                       John Wiley & Sons, 2009.

Katherine   *More than Title IX: How Equity in
Hanson, Vivian   Education Has Shaped the Nation.*
Guilfoy, and   Lanham, MD: Rowman & Littlefield,
Sarita Pillai   2009.

Eric A. Hanushek   *Schoolhouses, Courthouses, and
and Alfred A.   Statehouses: Solving the
Lindseth   Funding-Achievement Puzzle in
                       America's Public Schools.* Princeton,
                       NJ: Princeton University Press, 2009.

Chester Hartman   *The Integration Debate: Competing
and Gregory D.   Futures for American Cities.* New
Squires, eds.   York, NY: Routledge, 2010.

E.D. Hirsch Jr.   The *Making of Americans: Democracy
                       and Our Schools.* New Haven, CT:
                       Yale University Press, 2009.

Veda Jairrels   *African Americans and Standardized
                       Tests: The Real Reason for Low Test
                       Scores.* Sauk Village, IL: African
                       American Images, 2009.

Amanda Walker   *Objectifying Measures: The
Johnson   Dominance of High-Stakes Testing and
                       the Politics of Schooling.* Philadelphia,
                       PA: Temple University Press, 2009.

Kim Marshall · *Rethinking Teacher Supervision and Evaluation: How to Work Smart, Build Collaboration, and Close the Achievement Gap.* San Francisco, CA: Jossey-Bass, 2009.

Thomas McCarthy · *Race, Empire, and the Idea of Human Development.* New York: Cambridge University Press, 2009.

Charles Murray · *Real Education: Four Simple Truths for Bringing America's Schools Back to Reality.* New York: Crown Forum, 2008.

Linda F. Nathan · *The Hardest Questions Aren't on the Test: Lessons from an Innovative Urban School.* Boston, MA: Beacon Press, 2009.

Pedro A. Noguera · *The Trouble with Black Boys: And Other Reflections on Race, Equity, and the Future of Public Education.* San Francisco, CA: Jossey-Bass, 2008.

Colin Ong-Dean · *Distinguishing Disability: Parents, Privilege, and Special Education.* Chicago, IL: University of Chicago Press, 2009.

Rod Paige and Elaine Witty · *The Black-White Achievement Gap: Why Closing It Is the Greatest Civil Rights Issue of Our Time.* New York: American Management Association, 2009.

Susan Pinker   *The Sexual Paradox: Men, Women,*
                      and the Real Gender Gap. New York:
                      Scribner, 2008.

Michael A. Rebell   *Courts and Kids: Pursuing Educational*
                      Equity Through the State Courts.
                      Chicago, IL: University of Chicago
                      Press, 2009.

David Sadker,   *Still Failing at Fairness: How Gender*
Myra Sadker, and   *Bias Cheats Girls and Boys in School*
Karen Zittleman   *and What We Can Do About It.* New
                      York: Scribner, 2009.

Joseph Tobin, Yeh   *Preschool in Three Cultures Revisited:*
Hsueh, and   *China, Japan, and the United States.*
Mayumi Karasawa   Chicago, IL: University of Chicago
                      Press, 2009.

Joyce L.   *Patterns and Profiles of Promising*
VanTassel-Baska,   *Learners from Poverty.* Waco, TX:
ed.   Prufrock Press, 2009.

Tony Wagner   *The Global Achievement Gap: Why*
                      Even Our Best Schools Don't Teach the
                      New Survival Skills Our Children
                      Need—and What We Can Do About
                      It. New York: Basic Books, 2008.

Index

Voucher programs, housing, 99, 104

Voucher programs, schools, 49
do not narrow the achievement gap, 193–200
narrow the achievement gap, 183–192
See also School choices

W

Washington, D.C.
charter school achievement, 101
low achievement, 100, 101
school choice programs, 49–53, 193, 194–200

What America Can Learn from School Choice in Other Countries (Coulson), 183–192

White/minority dichotomy, 30, 32, 33, 36, 102

White students
dropout factors, 33, 34
privilege and social capital, 80–84, 177, 182
standardized test scores, 24, 57, 114

Whitman, David, 103

Williams, Khadijah, 19, 20

Winant, Howard, 176, 177

Wing, Jean Yonemura, 78–87

Witnesses to crime, 106, 107–111

Wolf, Patrick, 193–200

Women in science and engineering, 201–209, 210–220

Work-life balance, 205, 207

Working-class families. *See* Low-income families

Writing
boys' subject preferences, 118
student testing/performance, 86, 113–114, 189